The
HOLLYWOOD
BOWL

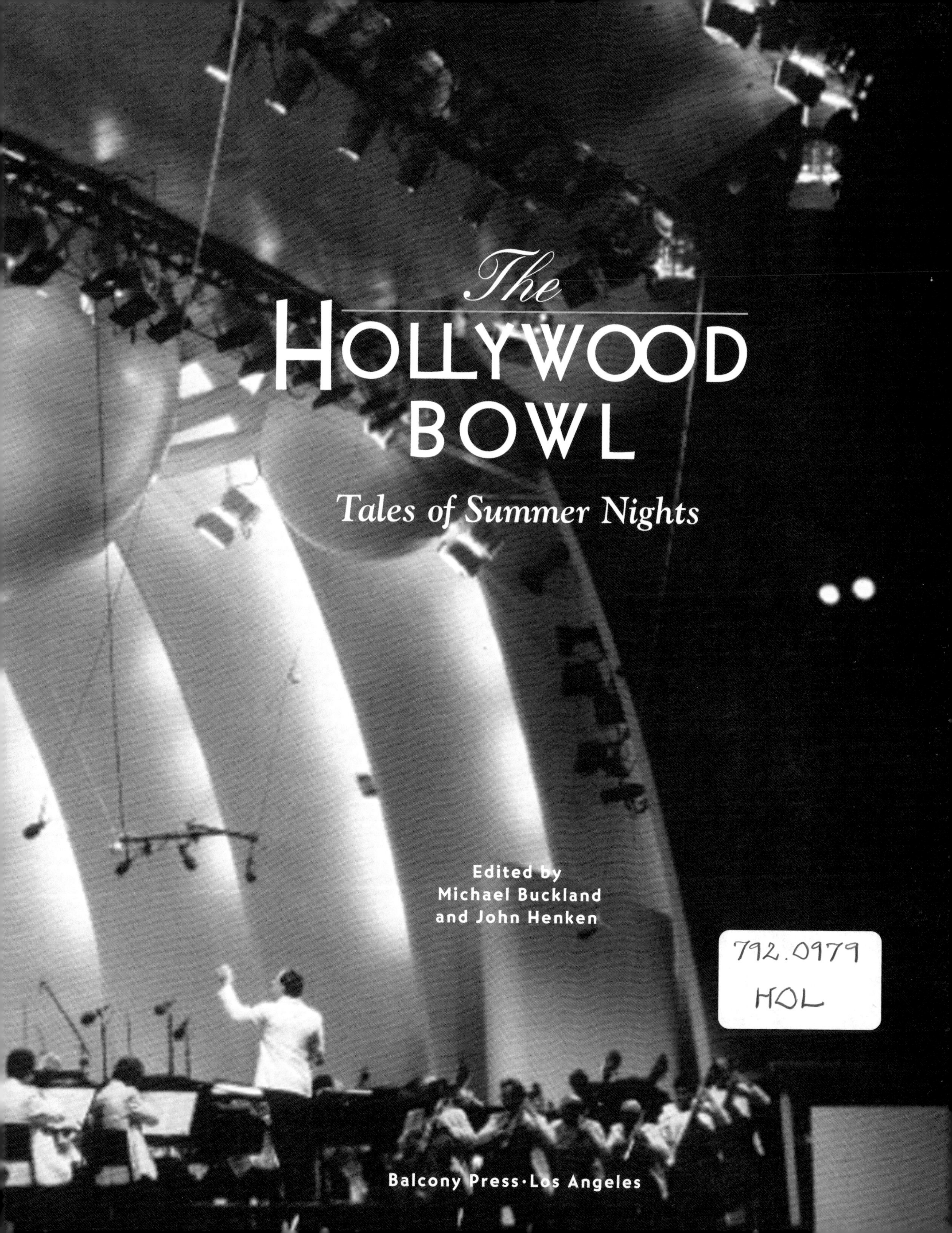

The
HOLLYWOOD
BOWL

Tales of Summer Nights

**Edited by
Michael Buckland
and John Henken**

Balcony Press·Los Angeles

This book is dedicated to the memory of Robert "Capt'n Bob" Di Vall (1921 − 1993), who played principal trumpet for the Los Angeles Philharmonic from 1951 to 1981. The rare spiritual quality of his tone distinguished his many solo appearances. Audiences were frequently spellbound by the clarity of his playing.

A native of Los Angeles, Bob loved the Hollywood Bowl and had the highest regard for his fellow musicians. This book, inspired by his integrity and good humor, reflects Bob's commitment to the Bowl.

Contents

FOREWORD

BY ERNEST FLEISCHMANN

I first visited the Hollywood Bowl in 1957. The program was all-Tchaikovsky, and neither the conductor nor the soloist (in "the" piano concerto) was able to lift the performances above dull routine. There were no fireworks and the sound emerging from the shell was gray and tinny. And yet, just as I will never forget the disappointing musical experience, I will always remember that magical feeling engendered by the velvet sky, the caressing air, the communal silence of thousands concentrating on the music.

Surely, only someone totally devoid of feelings will be unaffected by the Bowl's uniquely festive atmosphere, and only a curmudgeon of the most misanthropic sort (a music critic, perhaps?) will allow any perceived shortcomings on stage to interfere with that sense of otherworldly euphoria. Of course, technological advances have helped to enhance the quality of the actual sounds that reach today's audiences. And the performances themselves tend nowadays to be considerably more accomplished than the one I encountered on my first visit. There is probably no other place on earth where, within an urban area, 18,000 people can gather in a natural amphitheater, oblivious to the pressures of the city just outside their park-like sanctuary. A blessed oasis, where Bruno Walter and Igor Stravinsky, Ella Fitzgerald and Benny Goodman, Jascha Heifetz and Artur Rubinstein have enthralled huge audiences, just as Esa-Pekka Salonen and Simon Rattle, Ray Charles and Elton John, Yo-Yo Ma and Valery Gergiev entrance their audiences today.

As my tenure with the Bowl and the Los Angeles Philharmonic is nearing its end, I reflect with pleasure and gratitude on my good fortune at having been privileged to spend well over a third of the Bowl's (and my own) life caring for this wondrous place and this great orchestra. There is much glorious music still to be made, and many structural improvements still to be effected, ensuring that my successor will have a marvelously challenging and, I am certain, deeply satisfying time of it.

Meanwhile, there are hundreds of people, from John Mauceri, hero of our Hollywood Bowl Orchestra, to former County Supervisor Ed Edelman and present Supervisor Zev Yaroslavsky, from Bill Wilson (Mr. Hollywood Bowl Stage) and Pat Moore to Ed Tom (whose miracle work has kept the complex operation of the Bowl functioning so smoothly and efficiently), whom I want to thank most warmly for their totally devoted and incredibly efficient labors on behalf of this amazing summer festival. And there are three colleagues who have stood by my side and given of themselves unselfishly, wisely, energetically, and enthusiastically to help create all those hugely enjoyable events that go to make up every Bowl season: the late Jaye Rubanoff (Philharmonic manager from 1960 to 1978), Robert Harth (general manager 1979 to 1989), and the Bowl's present general manager, the indefatigable Anne Parsons.

Much hard work has gone into the making of this book, and I would particularly like to thank Dennis Bade and Michael Buckland for their invaluable editorial assistance. Above all, much gratitude is due to the Patroness Committee of the Hollywood Bowl and especially their president, Bee Jay Di Vall, for their bounteous generosity, without which it would not have been possible for this book to be published.

To all of them and to everyone whose generous contributions are helping to sustain the Bowl and the Philharmonic, I want to say a resounding thank you: you deserve to be extremely proud of the vitally important part you have played in the success of the Hollywood Bowl, the Los Angeles Philharmonic, and the Hollywood Bowl Orchestra.

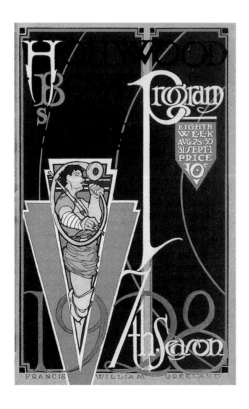

A BOWL RESOUNDING

BY JOHN HENKEN

There may be some sort of natural compensation in the fact that music, so ephemeral in the moment of performance, lingers so powerfully in the memory. The Hollywood Bowl, with its countless concerts, in recordings and films, and through radio and television broadcasts, has long since reached critical mass in our collective cultural memory. With its distinctive architecture and beautiful setting, the Hollywood Bowl has become an immediately recognizable international symbol.

At the beginning of the Bowl story, however, its subsequent renown could hardly have been imagined. That characteristic shell was still years away, and pageantry, arts education, and community events loomed larger than symphonic music in the minds of many of the original developers of the Bowl.

Those founders were a diverse lot, but that very diversity has proven to be a cornerstone of the Bowl's enduring cultural strength. From a range of artistic dreams and personal ambitions has come a pluralistic institution that is an icon, celebrated world-wide for the communal enjoyment of the performing arts.

Pre-eminent among the early leaders of what would become the Hollywood Bowl were Christine Weatherill Stevenson and Artie Mason Carter. Stevenson was a Philadelphia heiress, a theosophist, arts patron, and sometime dramatist. It was her activities on behalf of a proposed cycle of seven plays about religious prophets that led to the formation of a theater association and, ultimately, the purchase of the property on which the Bowl was developed. When she died unexpectedly in 1922 she had already split off from others who were moving toward the Bowl as we now know it. Her *Pilgrimage Play*, depicting the life of Christ, gave its name to the Pilgrimage Theater (now the John Anson Ford Amphitheatre, the home of Chamber Music Under the Stars, as well as drama, dance, pop, and jazz music events), on property she acquired on the east side of the Cahuenga Pass, opposite the Bowl.

Artur Rubinstein and Izler Solomon.

Carter was a graduate of two American music schools, a student of Theodor Leschetizky in Vienna, and the charismatic leader of the Hollywood Community Sing. Founded in 1917 on the patriotic fervor of the American entry into World War I, the Hollywood Community Sing was an immediate popular success. It was through Carter and the Sing that the Los Angeles Philharmonic, established in 1919, entered the Hollywood Bowl story.

An Easter sunrise service first brought the Hollywood Community Sing and the Los Angeles Philharmonic together, although *not* at the Bowl. In 1920 Carter invited the new orchestra to join the Sing for an Easter service in Hollywood, at what is now Barnsdall Park. The following year the service moved to the Bowl site, again with the Sing and the Philharmonic; the featured soloist was soprano Elizabeth Rothwell, wife of Philharmonic Music Director Walter Henry Rothwell.

"I remember well the first Easter Sunrise Service held in the Hollywood Bowl," Miriam Ziegler recalled in 1993. "I was a ten-year-old choir singer, under the direction of Hugo Kirchhofer.... The first Easter service was directed and presented from a small wooden platform. There were wooden benches to seat about 800 people. The rest of the people spread blankets on the ground and worshipped picnic-style.... Before this program, on a Saturday, the children's choir met to plant the lovely fir trees you now see towering in a small forest to your left as you face the Bowl stage."

Los Angeles was not as culturally bereft as is popularly imagined. In addition to the Easter services and community sings, early events at the Bowl site included festivals of black community and church choirs in 1919; a Thanksgiving Sing in 1920, with a pageant *The Landing of the Pilgrims* directed by Lionel Barrymore; a performance of Mendelssohn's *Elijah* in 1921, with John Smallman conducting the Los Angeles Oratorio Society; a series of Shakespeare plays in 1921, including *A Midsummer Night's Dream* with Mendelssohn's music and the Denishawn and Marion Morgan

dancers; weekly concerts by the 63-piece Greater Los Angeles Municipal Band during the summer of 1921; and an Armistice Day Mothers' Peace Service, featuring contralto Ernestine Schumann-Heink, on November 11, 1921.

In 1922 the Philharmonic returned to the Bowl for an Easter sunrise service, and that summer the concert series that would become known as "Symphonies Under the Stars" was inaugurated. The organizational road to Symphonies Under the Stars was paved by an often fractious group of Hollywood real-estate developers and businessmen — most prominent among them Charles E. Toberman — who controlled the property after the departure of Stevenson. But the vision was Carter's, shared and encouraged by musical entrepreneur and activist Frederick W. Blanchard, who had opened a music store in Los Angeles in 1896.

"Big musical projects are not impossible to put through, provided you get the people themselves to work and divide the financial burden," Carter proclaimed. "We raised the first thousands by popular subscription. Then see how interested they all were in the Bowl, because it was their own! In no other way than by sharing the responsibility can we make music the veritable possession of the people."

Carter indeed took her vision before the people, including the thousand members of the Hollywood Community Sing. She solicited support and raised money at the Easter sunrise service in 1922. When funds ran out midway through the inaugural season, the business minds proposed replacing the symphony programs with cheaper band concerts. Carter again took the problem before the audience, and raised enough money to see the symphony season completed.

With Rothwell engaged in New York that summer, and opposed to the project anyway, musical leadership for the first season — labeled "Hollywood Bowl Summer Popular Concerts" on the programs — fell to Alfred Hertz. The German-born conductor of the San Francisco Symphony proved an inspired choice. Always something of a maverick, he conducted at the Metropolitan Opera in New York the first *Parsifal* ever given outside Bayreuth, earning the enmity of Cosima Wagner. He also conducted the first operas by American composers performed at the Met, and under his leadership the San Francisco Symphony was one of the first American orchestras to accept women players and to record. Hertz was also the first conductor in the United States to lead a regular concert series on radio, the "Standard Oil Symphony Hour" (1932-36).

From top left:
Arapahoe Native Americans take part in a 1925 event at the Bowl.

Hugo Kirchhofer leads the Hollywood Community Sing at the Bowl in 1921.

An African-American chorus numbering over 400 sang at the Bowl on July 12, 1926.

The first Easter sunrise service at the Hollywood Bowl, in 1921, with the Los Angeles Philharmonic, and founder Willam Andrews Clark, Jr., soprano Elizabeth Rothwell, and conductor Walter Henry Rothwell on the podium.

Alfred Hertz leading a 1923 rehearsal at the Bowl.

Alfred Hertz with Artie Mason Carter in 1924.

French composer Charles Koechlin, winner of the 1929 Hollywood Bowl Composition Prize, shows his score to composer Gertrude Ross at the Bowl.

Hertz' inaugural Bowl program, Tuesday evening, July 11, 1922, began with Wagner's Overture to *Rienzi*, the *Andante cantabile* movement from Tchaikovsky's Symphony No. 5, and (unspecified) Hungarian Dances by Brahms. After intermission came the Suite No. 1 from Grieg's *Peer Gynt* music, and Fritz Kreisler's *Liebesleid* and *Liebesfreud*. The concert ended with Rossini's Overture to *William Tell*.

"Establishing a new ideal in the popularizing of music, the first of the series of summer concerts, under the auspices of the Community Park and Art Association, was given last night at the Hollywood Bowl," began Edwin Schallert in his *Los Angeles Times* review. "An orchestra of eighty-odd pieces, under the inspiring baton of Alfred Hertz, was the means of obtaining the desired objective, and the resultant 'harmony of sweet sound' pervading the still California evening air, brought an elusively poetic spell to nearly 5,000 listeners who gathered in the midst of the shadowed hills."

The second concert of the season shows that a propensity for calendar-inspired, thematic programs was a feature of the Bowl from birth. It offered French music by Auber, Bizet, Delibes, and Saint-Saëns (the Piano Concerto No. 2, with the unjustly forgotten virtuosa Olga Steeb the soloist), in honor of Bastille Day. "About 4,000 persons, composing a very attentive audience, were present last night, and by their applause showed plainly that these Bowl concerts are appreciated," wrote William Foster Elliot in the *Los Angeles Times*. "They deserve to be. The charm of being able to sit under the stars and listen to the sort of music Mr. Hertz is able to provide is an experience that must be felt to be appreciated. But I should think that no one after feeling it once would care to let it stop at that."

Later that first season came Spanish- and Russian-themed programs. There was a "Pasadena Day" featuring the Pasadena Community Orchestra and Arthur Farwell, a "University of California Night," a Charles Wakefield Cadman program, several children's concerts, and a Sunday afternoon performance of Rossini's *Stabat mater* with the City Club Ensemble (and the incongruous notice above the bill, "Dancing Immediately After the Program Under Auspices of Valada Girls Club, Hollywood").

Hertz also scheduled a concert of audience requests, asking concertgoers to send him (at the Beverly Hills Hotel) by August 12 a postcard listing their three favorite works from the season. The most frequently named works — the *William Tell* Overture, Schubert's "Unfinished" Symphony, two of Brahms' Hungarian Dances, Tchaikovsky's *Marche slav*, the ballet music from Massenet's *Le Cid*, and Wagner's *Tannhäuser* Overture and "Ride of the Valkyries" — were given August 15, just three days after Hertz received the final votes.

A charismatic leader, Hertz did much to make the symphonic agenda at the Bowl the popular success it quickly became. "I believe that I have done more to spread the gospel of good music during the last ten weeks than in all my life before," he commented at the end of the season.

In her autobiography, *Dance to the Piper*, Agnes de Mille offered this powerful recollection of the Bowl's first years that she experienced when she returned to produce an evening of original dance at the Bowl in 1935:

"This was the Bowl cratering up into the ringing sky, my mother's Bowl. (Hadn't she and Artie Mason Carter, their hats askew, dashed home to say you could hear a fifty-cent piece drop in any quarter of it?) During the first summer's performances I sat four nights a week on a blanket in the sagebrush. The next summer there were wooden benches, but the spring rain had rotted them and they tilted back on their moorings so we sat with our feet in the air staring straight into the stars. In the mornings, the hot, expansive mornings, I had permission to attend rehearsals and listened to 'Papa' Alfred Hertz put the boys through their paces. I was present when Galli-Curci rehearsed, standing very tiny in a white silk coat and holding an adorable little flowered cretonne parasol over her face lest she faint. When she finished, all the musicians beat their bows on the stands and I was so overcome I had to rush to buy an ice-cream soda to settle my feelings, but found I could not swallow it. The night before I entered the university Hertz played [Wagner's] Valhalla music and my heart nearly burst within me. So much of my inner life had transpired in musical experience, so much of that music had first been heard here!

"In 1924, at the head of the long road we had just plodded up [with her dancers in 1935], there once stood a large papier-mâché bowl, and Mother and the stars she commandeered, Wallace Reid, Milton Sills, Conrad Nagel, Thomas Meighan, called for pennies as the audience streamed out. 'Give your pennies to buy the Bowl! Pay off the mortgage of the Bowl!' The mortgage was burned by Artie Carter on stage the last night of the first season. Mother had stood by that bowl every night until

Luminaries of the early Bowl: (l-r) Harriet Clay Penman, Gertrude Ross, Mrs. Alfred Hertz, Dr. Hertz, Carrie Jacobs Bond, Charles Wakefield Cadman, Phillipe de Lacey, Artie Mason Carter, E.J. "Grandma" Wakeman, Mrs. Leiland Atherton Irish.

A crowd going up Peppertree Lane in 1922.

A billboard for the 1926 season of "Symphonies Under the Stars."

the audience had left, and then had taken her group home for hot chocolate and cookies."

Musical leadership of the second season, in 1923, was entrusted to Emil Oberhoffer, another German-born conductor, who had just retired as director of the Minneapolis Symphony. (When Rothwell died suddenly in 1927, it was Oberhoffer who led the Philharmonic for the remainder of the season.)

The third season saw the return of Hertz, who went on to become a Bowl fixture, conducting his 100th concert in 1934, his final season there. Though he was often simply a guest conductor, this period might be called the Hertz era, and a noble one it was. Guest conductors in 1924, for example, included Ernest Bloch leading his own *Three Jewish Poems*.

Repertory, indeed, was hardly the provincial tried-and-true it is sometimes imagined to have been. In 1925 a young Fritz Reiner brought Stravinsky's *Petrushka* Suite, *Fireworks*, and *Firebird* Suite, Honegger's *Pacific 231*, Falla's *El amor brujo* Suite, and Rieti's Concerto for Woodwinds — then all shockingly new music — to the first weeks of the season, and won great acclaim and popularity in the process. That same summer Sir Henry Wood gave Holst's *Planets*, Ethel Smyth's *On the Cliffs of Cornwall*, Vaughan Williams' *London* Symphony, Elgar's *Enigma Variations*, and Turina's *Procesión del Rocio* their Bowl premieres; Howard Hanson conducted his tone poem *Lux Aeterna* and his *Nordic* Symphony; and Ethel Leginska became the first woman to conduct a regular orchestral concert at the Bowl, with a program that included Beethoven's Symphony No. 7, Weber's Op. 11 Piano Concerto with herself the soloist, and her own *Nursery Rhymes* for soprano and chamber orchestra. That summer there was also recent music by Bloch, Deems Taylor, and John Alden Carpenter, among others.

Eugene Goossens described the Bowl experience of that era from a conductor's point of view in an article he wrote for *The Gramophone*, published in 1930. Note the assumption that "everyone" among the British magazine's readership would have heard of the Hollywood Bowl, only eight years after symphonic concerts began there.

"Everyone has heard of the Hollywood Bowl, but few people realize the acoustic marvels of this enormous natural amphitheatre in the California hills, where the metaphorical pin dropped on the orchestra stage can be heard on the hill-top a quarter of a mile away. During eight weeks of cloudless summer weather, concerts are held in the Bowl on four evenings out of seven. And the sensation of conducting a fine orchestra under that marvelous blue vault studded with blazing stars, with an audience of twenty or thirty thousand thronging the darkness of the hillsides, remains unforgettable and indescribable.

Top: Aaron Copland, at the
Hollywood Bowl in 1928 to
play the West Coast premiere
of his Piano Concerto.

Left: Fritz Reiner, in rehearsal
at the Bowl in 1925.

Rear: Arnold Schoenberg
wrote his *Fanfare for a Bowl
Concert* for Leopold Stokowski,
who gave its premiere at the
Bowl in 1945.

Patriotic wartime concert,
June 1945.

The KFI equipment for the
Bowl's first radio broadcast in
1927.

"Immediately before the concert begins, the brilliant searchlights illuminating the amphitheatre are switched out. Except for the powerful light focused on the orchestra shell, the Bowl is in complete darkness. Walking out onto the platform, one sees nothing but a few pale blurs of faces immediately below the stage, and only the sudden flash of a smoker's match far up the hillside betrays the presence of the waiting multitudes. The uncanny consciousness of those thousands of invisible eyes focused on the small of one's back, the unique sense of contact with and response from that unseen audience, has made those California nights the most inspiring of memories."

For Aaron Copland, memories of the West Coast premiere of his jazz-influenced Piano Concerto at the Hollywood Bowl in 1928 were not quite so idyllic. "There at rehearsals the musicians actually hissed," the composer recalled in his autobiography. "The conductor, Albert Coates, was distraught: 'Boys! Boys, please!' he pleaded, pointing to me at the piano. 'He's one of *us*!' "

Non-symphonic concerts, dance, drama, and community events continued to hold special places on the Bowl agendas. In 1927, for example, the 500 voices of the Los Angeles Oratorio Society sang with the orchestra on two programs, Hertz conducted a program featuring dancers Ruth St. Denis and Ted Shawn, there was a series of Sunday afternoon American Legion concerts, a production of Reginald De Koven's operetta *Robin Hood*, and a group of Native Americans leased the Bowl for "Inter-tribal Indian Ceremonials" in September. The California Federation of Women's Clubs and the Southern California Inter-Scholastic Debating and Oratorical League also held events at the Bowl.

That was also the year Gershwin's *Rhapsody in Blue* had its first performance at the Bowl. By that season the amphitheater had already become a summer entertainment mecca. Season boxes were held by such artists, socialites, moguls, and celebrities as Aline Barnsdall, Charles Wakefield Cadman, William Andrews Clark, Jr., Mr. and Mrs. Cecil B. DeMille, Mr. and Mrs. Edward L. Doheny, Mr. and Mrs. Douglas Fairbanks, Sid Grauman, Louis B. Mayer, and Adela Rogers St. John.

1927 also marked the first radio broadcast from the Bowl. Radio would play an important role at the Bowl for many years. "Hollywood Bowl Night," which became one of the most popular programs offered by Armed Forces Radio Service during World War II and the following years, was broadcast from stations around the world and distributed to military hospitals and ships.

The Hertz years saw the establishment of the Bowl Auditions, which gave local artists performance opportunities, and a Bowl Composition Prize. Grace Elliot Gibson won the first award in 1928 (with an honorable mention to Dane Rudhyar), and Charles Koechlin won the following year for *Pagan Joy* (from *Etudes antiques*).

Two dramatic events dominate the last years of the Hertz era. On August 9, 1928, Percy Grainger was married to the Swedish poet Ella Viola Ström on the stage of the Bowl, following a concert he conducted which featured the world premiere of his own "Bridal Song," *To a Nordic Princess*. The following night Grainger was back at the Bowl as the soloist in Grieg's Piano Concerto, and he conducted the concert the next night. After that, he and his bride departed for their honeymoon, a hiking tour of Glacier National Park.

In 1933 came *l'affaire Slonimsky*. That was a troubled season, one among many in those years in terms of money and concomitant power struggles. Nicolas Slonimsky, that irrepressible musical iconoclast, was said to have been engaged to lead the entire 1933 summer season on the strength of good reports of his winter season concerts with the Los Angeles Philharmonic, December 29 and 30, 1932. To the surprise and horror of all, he introduced "modern" music to the Bowl. His contract was then alleged to have been bought out, with Slonimsky being released after only two weeks.

The programs and contemporary documents from 1933, however, suggest something slightly less dramatic. Neither modern music nor Slonimsky himself took either the Bowl authorities or its public entirely by surprise. Advance stories in the press took notice of Slonimsky's reputation, and even evinced polite anticipation. There is every indication that his time at the Bowl was fixed before he ever raised his baton in Cahuenga Pass. Indeed, Hertz conducted the season opener, and Sir Hamilton Harty followed Slonimsky in clearly scheduled sequence.

Otto Klemperer.

Artur Rubinstein and Sir
Thomas Beecham.

Top left: Serge Koussevitzky.
Top right: Zubin Mehta with
Mstislav Rostropovich.
Bottom: Carlo Maria Giulini
in rehearsal.

Bruno Walter, Leonard Bernstein,
Antonia Brico.

In the rather wild context of Bowl programming of the day, Slonimsky's agendas were not exceptionally outré, and even had decidedly populist elements. Terror lurked on his third program in the form of Varèse's *Ionisation*, but compensating for that was a bit of Mozart juvenilia, Scriabin's "Divine Poem" Third Symphony, Bach's Piano Concerto in D minor with Lillian Steuber, and Richard Strauss' *Till Eulenspiegel*.

Reviews did become increasingly patronizing and dismissive, but historically Slonimsky's greatest disadvantage probably was having been hired by the losers in the management crisis of the summer. From the beginning there had been tensions between the professional business interests and the arts idealists in the development of the Bowl and its programs. The off-again, on-again season of 1933 saw the rancorous climax of a struggle which had pitted imported management professionals against the long-time, local volunteers. It featured labor strife, the threat of moving the concerts to the Greek Theater, and even rival radio stations vying for broadcast rights to Bowl concerts (and the lucrative Standard Oil advertising). After much ado, the orchestra was back in action, KFI was broadcasting (without Standard Oil sponsorship), and the longtimers were restored to leadership. Most subsequently published accounts — Slonimsky's own reports aside — came from sources close to the victors, and Slonimsky retroactively became a symbol of all the fearful things presumed to have gone wrong under the earlier administration.

Despite the Great Depression there was, between the end of the Hertz years and the beginning of World War II, a golden era of dance and opera at the Bowl, and path-breaking events, such as Benny Goodman's 1939 non-subscription jazz concert. The great conductors and instrumentalists were still there, of course (including the incipient great, such as the nine-year-old conductor Lorin Maazel in 1939), but those were the years of Jan Peerce, Lily Pons, Kirsten Flagstad, Lotte Lehmann, and Lawrence Tibbett, among many others. Dance events featured Agnes de Mille, Albertina Rausch, Lester Horton, and Michio Ito, while among the operas presented were *Aida, Lohengrin, La traviata, The Bartered Bride, Pagliacci, Eugene Onegin, Il trovatore, Madama Butterfly, The Barber of Seville, Cavalleria rusticana,* and *Martha.* Many were staged, perhaps most memorably the 1938 *Walküre,* with the Valkyries riding real horses on the hills behind the Bowl shell.

Dance and voice continued to be major forces during the war years, as the Bowl at times became one big canteen. To the names above could be added Lauritz Melchior, Grace Moore, Paul Robeson, Jarmila Novotna, Helen Traubel, Risë Stevens, Marian Anderson, Ezio Pinza, the Nijinska Ballet, and the Ballet Russe de Monte Carlo.

With so many traditional performance venues out of commission during the war, the Bowl saw a parade of many of the greatest artists of the time. In 1941 Vladimir Horowitz made his Bowl debut. Already notoriously demanding about performing conditions, Horowitz had never played concerts outdoors before. He discovered, as he later recalled, that he "sounded good there," and he returned the following season. That year he was drawn as much by his friendship with Sergei Rachmaninoff as by the Bowl's reputation and the exigencies of the time. Rachmaninoff gave two performances of his Piano Concerto No. 2 at the Bowl in July and a few weeks later Horowitz played the composer's Piano Concerto No. 3, under William Steinberg. At the conclusion of the performance, Rachmaninoff walked onstage, took Horowitz by the hand and told the pianist that this was how he had always dreamed his concerto should be played — "the greatest moment of my life," Horowitz later proclaimed. Rachmaninoff died shortly afterwards at his new home in Hollywood.

For war-years star power, consider the 22nd season in 1943, which proudly hosted Captain Meredith Willson, Private Leonard Pennario, and Corporal Bronislaw Gimpel. The conductors included Sir Thomas Beecham, Albert Coates, Eugene Goossens, Ferde Grofé, José Iturbi, Otto Klemperer, Miklós Rózsa, Igor Stravinsky, George Szell, Bruno Walter, and Paul Whiteman; numbered among the pianists were Claudio Arrau, Jakob Gimpel, Oscar Levant, Amparo Navarro, and Artur Rubinstein. This was the season that Frank Sinatra made his Bowl debut — although the idea of a crooner at the hallowed Bowl stirred some controversy, Sinatra quite successfully established the

Frank Sinatra onstage at the Bowl.

Sir Simon Rattle.

Dorothy Chandler at the
Hollywood Bowl, 1954.

kind of symphonic pop now enshrined at the Bowl — and the dancers included Ballet Theatre and flamenco legends Carmen Amaya and Antonio Triana.

The immediate post-war years continued much as before, although new stars increasingly made their presence felt. Leonard Bernstein had made his Bowl debut in 1944 (conducting Ballet Theatre performances of his *Fancy Free*, in its premiere season), and he was followed on the podium in later years by Serge Koussevitzky and Erich Leinsdorf, as well as Johnny Green, Xavier Cugat, Sigmund Romberg, Carmen Dragon, and Arthur Fiedler. Eugene Ormandy led the first West Coast performance of Mahler's monumental Symphony No. 8 at the Hollywood Bowl in 1948. Opera and dance events continued and a new chorus, the Roger Wagner Chorale, became a regular force.

Opera and stars have their price, however, and all the bills seemed to come due in 1951. The season opened with an unpopular, budget-busting production of *Die Fledermaus*, featuring Yvonne De Carlo in the trouser role of Prince Orlovsky. (The freely expressed distaste for what was purported to be an overly sophisticated rarity also puts the Slonimsky hysteria in context; dislike and distrust of the current Bowl management figured in this fiasco as they had in *l'affaire Slonimsky*.) A week later the season abruptly closed, bankrupt.

There was an international outcry of anguish, but the tragedy proved short-lived. Dorothy Buffum Chandler was elected to chair an "Emergency Committee." An heiress of heretofore under-utilized organizing drive and fund-raising acumen, she rallied broad-based support, including the donation of services by many artists. After missing little more than a week of programs, the Bowl reopened July 26 with a renewed commitment to the original principles of Symphonies Under the Stars, i.e., symphonic music for everyone. Ticket prices were reduced, audiences returned, and the post-*Fledermaus* season actually turned a profit.

In following seasons Chandler became president of the Bowl Association and oversaw the modernization of the physical plant and many improvements to the grounds, including the installation of a reflecting pool. Her contributions were honored at the last concert of the 1958 season with the

premiere of "The Dorothy Chandler Theme for Hollywood Bowl," a caril-
lon fanfare by Elinor Remick Warren which called concertgoers to their
seats for many years.

Artistic ambition did not vanish in post-crisis seasons. Opera and
dance remained regular features, although a shift from opera to oratorio
became apparent by the end of the '50s. Perhaps the most ambitious project of the decade was the very progressive Festival of the Americas in 1955
(the summer which also saw the first Disney night at the Bowl). The music
director for the five programs was Leonard Bernstein, who began on
August 16 with a program featuring Isaac Stern in Bernstein's *Serenade*,
Jennie Tourel in Lukas Foss' *Song of Songs* cantata, and Gregory Peck narrating Copland's *Lincoln Portrait*. The second program presented Martha
Graham and her company in *Diversion of Angels*, *Night Journey*, and
Appalachian Spring, while the third program found Carlos Chávez conduct-
ing the Philharmonic and soprano Bidu Sayão in music by Latino
composers. A jazz concert brought together Dave Brubeck, Buddy de
Franco, Billie Holiday, Pete Kelly, Lee Konitz, André Previn, Shorty
Rogers, Shelly Manne, and Cal Tjader, and the closing program of show
tunes and film music — with Bernstein the piano soloist in Gershwin's
Rhapsody in Blue — was labeled "Music for Everyone."

By the end of the '50s and into the '60s, the incipient Music Center
downtown began to occupy Bowl attention in the form of "Cornerstone
Concerts" benefits, another product of Dorothy Chandler's remarkable
energies. In a formidable display of virtuosity and sheer stamina, Van
Cliburn was the soloist for the 1959 pair (the year after his Tchaikovsky
Competition triumph), playing Beethoven's "Emperor" Concerto and
Prokofiev's No. 3 one night, returning three days later with the Schumann
Concerto and Rachmaninoff's No. 3.

Midori.

Although this might seem rather extraordinary, soloists playing two concertos were not
extremely rare at the Bowl. Oscar Levant, for example, gave the local premieres of Arthur Honegger's
Concertino, Gershwin's Second Rhapsody, and the Khachaturian Piano Concerto all on one program
in 1949, under Erich Leinsdorf. Levant also gave his first performance of the Tchaikovsky Piano
Concerto No. 1 at the Bowl, prefaced by the Grieg Concerto. Conducted by Ormandy, that 1947 program began with a Handel overture and had Brahms' Symphony No. 4 at the center, between the two
concertos.

"I remonstrated with Ormandy about the program," Levant recalled in *Memoirs of an Amnesiac*,
"and even Vladimir Horowitz came to my defense and said it was not an advantageous program for
the soloist. Ormandy was eager to conduct for me in those days because I was a big draw, but suddenly — in a spate of self-revelation — he said, 'I did not come out here to be an accompanist'."

A new conductor, Zubin Mehta, began to dominate the podium, making his debut in 1961,
before he was appointed music director of the Los Angeles Philharmonic at the beginning of the
winter season. Mehta's first Bowl programs were comprised of Lukas Foss' *Ode for Orchestra*, the
Rachmaninoff Piano Concerto No. 3 (Byron Janis the soloist), and Berlioz' *Symphonie fantastique* on
August 1, followed by Rossini's Overture to *The Barber of Seville*, Beethoven's "Emperor" Concerto
(Benno Moiseiwitsch the soloist, in *his* Bowl debut), Kodály's *Dances from Galánta*, and Ravel's *La valse*.

"I don't think that there has been an important musical artist in the 20th century, either clas-
sical or pop, who has not enthralled thousands at the Hollywood Bowl," Mehta says. "It is 'as
American as apple pie.' To be invited to appear on its stage is as prestigious to the West Coast as
Carnegie Hall is to the East."

André Watts.

John Mauceri.

The years immediately following proved difficult ones for the Bowl in terms of maintaining audiences and financial support. Many reasons have been advanced — the building of the Music Center was a distraction on several levels, the Bowl Association became embroiled in several lawsuits (fighting the development of high-rise apartments around the Bowl and defending the *Pilgrimage Play* which it was playing across the Cahuenga Pass at the Pilgrimage Theater), troubles with the aging shell, and the general social upheavals of the '60s. The spectrum of Bowl offerings became, if anything, even broader, but achievements remained high. The 1962 summer, for example, saw the celebration of Stravinsky's 80th birthday (with the composer and Robert Craft conducting), the first national telecast of a Bowl concert (a Tchaikovsky program conducted by André Kostelanetz with pianist Lorin Hollander, taped on July 24 by KHJ-TV and aired on August 1), and the U.S. debut of Mexico's now-celebrated Ballet Folklórico.

Despite the accomplishments and the continued diversification of programs (guests, for example, ranged from The Beatles to the Royal Ballet, from Miles Davis to P.D.Q. Bach), the desired audience response was not forthcoming, and the institutional soul-searching again took on crisis over-tones. On July 11, 1966 (the 43rd birthday of symphonic concerts at the Hollywood Bowl), the

Hollywood Bowl Association and the Southern California Symphony Association merged. The move had long been discussed, and in retrospect seems an obvious one, the historical success of which is unarguable. At the time, though, the fear that the Bowl would become a summer step-child of the Philharmonic and the splendid new Music Center was keenly felt. Instead, both public and organizational support for the Bowl grew rapidly.

An artist new to the Bowl that summer of 1966 was violinist Itzhak Perlman, who has returned many times since. "I have had a lot of experience playing outdoors, but nothing is as special or exciting as playing the Hollywood Bowl. Looking at 18,000 people who are practically sitting in your lap is an experience that is unforgettable," says Perlman.

Perhaps the most far-reaching act of the newly merged associations was the hiring of Ernest Fleischmann in 1969 as both general director of the Hollywood Bowl and executive director of the Los Angeles Philharmonic. Born in Germany and trained in South Africa as both an accountant and a conductor, Fleischmann came to Los Angeles from stints in London as general manager of the London Symphony and as European director of the classical section of Columbia Records.

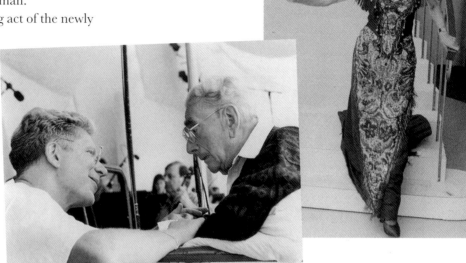

Much of what now seems most characteristic of the Bowl experience began under Fleischmann, and his impact was immediate. His first summer, for example, saw the establishment of a now-hallowed tradition — fireworks at the Bowl. The debut program was a Tchaikovsky Spectacular (Tchaikovsky programs, ending with the *1812 Overture*, had long been a Bowl staple *without* fireworks) on August 16, 1969, conducted by Zubin Mehta.

"I was amazed," Fleischmann says. "The so-called 'capital of show biz' had never used the facility to do the obvious." Pyrotechnics were added to the Independence Day and season finale programs in 1971, and have blossomed annually ever since.

Among Fleischmann's other early contributions to the Bowl were themed marathon programs, steady improvements to the sound system and the acoustics of the Bowl shell, and the inauguration of Open House at Hollywood Bowl, a daytime family festival-within-a-festival.

All of this was fully evident by the Bowl's "50th Birthday Superseason" of 1972, which featured Baroque, Beethoven, and Stravinsky marathons conducted by Lukas Foss, special "Day of New Music" and "Family Picnic" programs, pre-season pops conducted by John Green, a post-season "bonus week," and Open House at Hollywood Bowl.

The official opening program — on July 11, 1972, the 50th birthday of symphonic music at the Bowl — was a concert performance of *Aida*, conducted by James Levine, with Jessye Norman making her U.S. operatic debut in the title role. Levine also conducted Berlioz' *Romeo and Juliet* that summer, and a concert *Rigoletto* with a cast that included Louis Quilico in the title role, José Carreras as the Duke, Carol Neblett as Gilda, and Christine Weidinger, Claudine Carlson, Roger Patterson, Douglas Lawrence, and John Macurdy. At the Bowl for three weeks, Levine conducted other pro-

Left: John Mauceri welcomes composer Miklós Rózsa to a rehearsal of music from the Academy Award-winning score for *Ben-Hur*.
Right: Carol Channing practices her entrance for a Tribute to Jerry Herman.

Ernest Fleischmann with cellist Yo-Yo Ma.

grams that included the Fireworks Finale, and a Mozart/Mahler evening in which he also served as soloist, playing Mozart's sublime last Piano Concerto, No. 27 in B-flat, K. 595.

Other singers new to the Bowl in the '70s included Luciano Pavarotti and Montserrat Caballé. Conductors Carlo Maria Giulini, Simon Rattle, Michael Tilson Thomas, John Williams, André Previn, James DePreist, and Leonard Slatkin made their Bowl debuts, as did pianists André Watts, Radu Lupu, Emanuel Ax, Yefim Bronfman, and Alexander Toradze, violinist Pinchas Zukerman, cellists Lynn Harrell and Yo-Yo Ma, and flutists James Galway and Jean-Pierre Rampal. Mstislav Rostropovich made his Bowl debuts as both cellist and conductor, and Christoph Eschenbach appeared as both pianist and conductor. In 1979 Mikhail Baryshnikov gave three performances, and the Playboy Jazz Festival was inaugurated.

Perhaps the most significant innovation of the 1980s was the establishment of the Los Angeles Philharmonic Institute. The brainchild of Leonard Bernstein and Ernest Fleischmann, it was founded in 1981 with Bernstein and Daniel Lewis as artistic directors. Subsequently, Michael Tilson Thomas and Lynn Harrell headed the Institute. For ten seasons it provided world-class training for young musicians, both instrumentalists and conductors, a number of whom have since returned as accomplished and acclaimed professionals, including conductors Yakov Kreizberg, Keith Lockhart, and David Alan Miller.

After making a highly successful American debut with the Los Angeles Philharmonic the previous winter season, Esa-Pekka Salonen made his Hollywood Bowl debut in 1985, leading a Bernstein/Gershwin/ Sibelius agenda and a Beethoven program. Other conductors making Bowl debuts in the '80s included Yuri Temirkanov, Myung-Whun Chung, Charles Dutoit, and Herbert Blomstedt. Among the soloists making first appearances at the Bowl were pianists Andrea Lucchesini, Ivo Pogorelich, Krystian Zimerman, Dudley Moore, and Katia and Marielle Labèque, violinists Gidon Kremer, Joshua Bell, and Midori, clarinetist Richard Stoltzman, and singers Kiri Te Kanawa and Frederica Von Stade.

One of the most important debuts of the '90s was undoubtedly that of the Hollywood Bowl Orchestra under conductor John Mauceri, July 2, 3, and 4, 1991. Over the years, Bowl seasons had featured a number of ensembles that performed under names such as Hollywood Bowl Symphony, Hollywood Bowl "Pops" Orchestra, etc.; most of them were largely composed of Los Angeles Philharmonic musicians. The Hollywood Bowl Orchestra, founded in 1991, is an entirely separate ensemble, which has firmly planted hometown roots and developed an enviable international reputation as a result of its recordings and tours. Mauceri and the Hollywood Bowl Orchestra have also played an important role in the increasing emphasis on multimedia events at the Bowl, creating new fireworks programs and often incorporating film elements projected onto the Bowl's big screen.

In 1990, the Rodri Entertainment Group launched its Mariachi USA Festival, which has joined the Playboy Jazz Festival as one of the pillars of the pre-season events, which had long included activities as disparate as the Hollywood High School graduation ceremonies and performances by Circus Vargas (in the Bowl parking lot). The Bowl's close and enduring connection to the greater Los

Angeles community was also reflected in the first half of the 1990s through involvement in other festivals, as it hosted Peter Sellars-directed Los Angeles Festival events in 1990 and 1993, and World Cup Week in 1994. The latter opened with Van Cliburn and the Moscow Philharmonic in an unusual and ambitious program — Cliburn narrated Copland's *Lincoln Portrait* and was to play two concertos, as he had 35 years earlier. The evening turned dramatic when the pianist became indisposed in the course of the evening and replaced the Rachmaninoff Third Concerto with a series of solo encores. Other concerts of the week included the Los Angeles Philharmonic under John Williams with soloists Itzhak Perlman and Linda Ronstadt, and John Mauceri and the Hollywood Bowl Orchestra, with country star Garth Brooks, and in an "Arabian Night's Fantasy" fireworks program.

With the active participation of Esa-Pekka Salonen, music director of the Los Angeles Philharmonic, and the Hollywood Bowl Orchestra's John Mauceri, the Bowl continues to innovate while remaining committed to the founding ideals. New conductors in the 1990s range from Roger Norrington and Sian Edwards to Bobby McFerrin. Pianists Hélène Grimaud and Nikolai Demidenko, violinists Sarah Chang, Leila Josefowicz, Anne Akiko Meyers, Vadim Repin, and Maxim Vengerov, violist Yuri Bashmet, cellist Steven Isserlis, trumpeter Arturo Sandoval, percussionist Evelyn Glennie, soprano Jane Eaglen, and baritone Dmitri Hvorostovsky are numbered among the solo artists making significant Bowl debuts. Jazz and pop continue to flourish, and opera is exerting a renewed presence.

The Bowl experience — communal enjoyment of performing arts in an enchanting, park-like setting — has, if anything, been intensified. Programs to ease transportation and parking problems and to make the Bowl welcoming to persons with disabilities and from the diverse cultural and ethnic communities of Los Angeles, coupled with ticket prices that still start at $1 for many events, have made this unique cultural facility available to a continually growing audience. At mid-decade, the Bowl's physical plant is again undergoing renovations and improvements to meet the needs of this ever-changing, burgeoning audience, and the future seems to hold as much promise as the past does fulfillment. The faces are changing but the song remains the same — the very best of music and the performing arts in the widest variety.

Esa-Pekka Salonen in concert and rehearsing with violinist Gidon Kremer.

ARCHITECTURE FOR PERFORMANCE

BY CAROL MCMICHAEL REESE

The Hollywood Bowl became a Los Angeles institution in the 1920s, and by the end of the 1930s the Bowl was so successful that it was emulated both in form and spirit across the country. Chicago's Grant Park on the shore of Lake Michigan (1931) copied the Bowl's shell of 1929. Denver's Red Rocks amphitheater (1939) took up Hollywood's idea of outdoor performances in a spectacular natural setting. And there were other echoes of the Bowl's influence from the Humboldt Park Music Shell in Milwaukee (1934) to the Hatch Shell in Boston (1940). Architecture played — and still plays — a key role in defining performances at the Bowl and in giving them meaning.

The Bowl's founders were a group of supporters of the performing arts who believed in the civic value of open-air productions. Brought together by Christine Wetherill Stevenson, the Theater Arts Alliance incorporated in May 1919 with the stated goal of creating a "community park and art center." Their passion for establishing a site for outdoor performances stemmed from the widely-held idea that music, theater, and dance staged outdoors had unique power not only to entertain and educate, but also to build community spirit. Open-air performance was seen to undergird, if not advance, American democracy itself. As the art and theater critic Sheldon Cheney wrote in 1918 in *The Open-Air Theater*, "The drama of the indoor stage is unavoidably the art of the few... whereas the outdoor drama is distinctly social, communal, and national.... It draws large numbers of people into a common artistic pursuit, and in its symbolism and historic allusions it tends to awaken civic consciousness." The Hollywood Bowl would become a crucible in which the populist values that Cheney described were molded.

Well aware of the pace and direction of the Los Angeles area's urban development, the members of the Theater Arts Alliance made a savvy choice of a site for their proposed activities. Bolton Canyon lay very near the heart of commercial Hollywood — which was the intersection of Hollywood Boulevard and Highland Avenue — a mere half-mile hike up the hill. Moreover, Bolton Canyon opened directly off the Cahuenga Pass — a primary connector route between Los Angeles and the growing communities of the San Fernando Valley — so that it was accessible to residents of the entire region. Across Highland Avenue from Bolton Canyon, the subdivision of Whitley Heights (opened in

Frank Gehry's "architectural champagne cocktail."

Singer Anna Ruzena Sprotte auditions the acoustics of Bolton Canyon on a makeshift stage, 1919.

1918) offered graded and terraced lots with "ocean views" to homebuilders. But in the chaparral-covered canyon, where yucca, nopal, and sage grew wild on the ridges, and scrub oak, mesquite, and manzanita filled the ravine, nature and art would together find sanctuary.

In 1919, Hollywood residents were accustomed to traveling around the metropolitan area by light rail transit to events in the city's parks. With the opening of "The Park," as the Theater Arts Alliance christened Bolton Canyon, they could find cultural events closer to home. Theatergoers, music and art lovers, nature buffs, politicians, real estate developers, and civic boosters alike saw its potential and agreed that it would be a boon to the community.

In general, outdoor-theater advocates favored sites that were either sloped — providing a natural amphitheater — or were topographically dramatic, providing a spectacular natural backdrop. Bolton Canyon offered both: the raking hillside to the south could provide amphitheater seating that would look away from the lights of the city toward the "stage" of the canyon floor, and the opposite slope could be used for presenting spectacles with large supporting casts. Thus, the future Bowl site presented two of the three types of theatrical scenarios that Sheldon Cheney discussed. It could accommodate a "Modern Greek Theatre" with tiers of seats, an orchestra circle or pit, and an open, back-walled stage. It could also serve as a "Nature Theatre" with performances mounted on the

Above: Set design (1927) by
Lloyd Wright for the
production of *Robin Hood*
(Castle in Act III) at the Bowl.

Right: Preliminary design
(1927) by Lloyd Wright for a
pyramidal orchestra shell to
replace the Allied Architects'
shell of 1926.

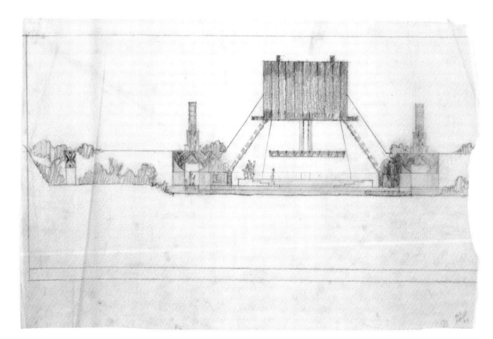

northerly ridge and hillside. Only a flat area large enough to provide what Cheney termed a "Garden Theatre" was lacking in Bolton Canyon.

The founders of the Bowl established it as a site where many different types of productions would engage audiences seeking a variety of experiences. Indeed, a wide panorama of events staged outdoors in Los Angeles in the early 20th century drew huge crowds. The Bowl site provided a congenial stage for productions in the movement known as "American Pageantry" which reenacted religious and historic themes. It also became the home of Los Angeles' best-attended Easter service in 1921, where it has "played" ever since [with two years off for construction in 1995 and 1996; also one year in the '30s].

The 1916 offering of Shakespeare's *Julius Caesar* in the natural amphitheater of Beachwood Canyon was revived in 1926 at the Bowl. *Julius Caesar* was one of the large spectaculars that made full use of the site as a "nature" theater, with a "forum" set on the canyon floor and "troops" encamped on the hillside behind.

The dynamism and popularity of contemporary open-air pageants and spectacles in Los Angeles led to the prediction that audiences would flock to the outdoor arena that the Bowl's founders imagined. Bolton Canyon could be a thrilling space in which to stage theater, music, and dance. Its success, however, depended upon achieving harmonious interaction among the natural environment, performances enacted there, and human presence in the landscape. The Bowl's founders called upon architecture to bring the three into a balanced relationship.

Controversy about how to resolve these factors arose as soon as the Theater Arts Alliance board commissioned San Francisco architect Louis Christian Mullgardt to prepare development plans in the summer of 1919. Mullgardt was highly regarded as the designer of the imposing central court of San Francisco's 1915 Panama-Pacific International Exposition in Golden Gate Park — an experience which must have seemed appropriate to the goal of building a community arts complex. Although board president Christine Stevenson paid Mullgardt's initial fees, she rejected his designs for their emphasis on "general entertainment" and neglect of her theatrical needs. After Stevenson's departure from the board, Mullgardt continued to be in contact with the group for several years, but the one-million-dollar price tag of his scheme exceeded their financial reach. In addition, some members of the alliance objected to Mullgardt's design, judging his plan too ornate for the natural character of Bolton Canyon. This early difference of opinion among the Bowl's leaders initiated a search for rapport between landscape and architecture that still continues.

Bringing the vision to fruition required not only capital for investment in architectural improvements but also substantial agreement about what they should be, who would design them, and which types of productions they would support. The Bowl survived its first three seasons on the income from gate receipts under the direction of pianist Artie Mason Carter but with no surplus or endowment for significant improvement. A leader of the Hollywood Community Sing, Carter dreamt of bringing symphonic music to the Bowl. Successful in 1922, she presided over the first series of "Symphonies Under the Stars," which the Los Angeles Philharmonic (founded 1919) played. In an effort to encourage community attendance, Carter insisted that tickets be priced at 25 cents, and although she attracted takers by the thousands, there was not enough in the Bowl's coffers to retire all the debts on the property, let alone begin major improvements.

Fortunately, her conductor, Alfred Hertz, embraced the challenge of directing in a largely unimproved outdoor amphitheater, which daunted the Philharmonic's first conductor, Walter Henry Rothwell. The ebullient, well-loved Hertz strengthened the Bowl's hold on the community. Wagner was Hertz's signature, and the bold strength of that composer's works played well in the immensity of the Bowl. Even as Hertz's presence gave a sense of stability and regularity to the Bowl's earliest seasons, however, the architectural environment retained a temporary quality.

For the initial season of "Symphonies Under the Stars," some landscape planting was undertaken, the hillside was graded, and simple wooden benches were built to provide seating. The musicians played on a temporary, wood-framed stage with a canvas roof and wing-walls accented by cylinders. In 1923, the Bowl's directors built 150 boxes. In 1924, they purchased land along the canyon entrance and built a backdrop for the stage that created a semblance of what Cheney had termed the "Garden Theatre." It had columned pergolas set against decorated walls and Greek urns to either side of the stage with a canvas roof. This structure survived only through the 1925 season, but its simple architectural elements symbolized two fundamental ideas about the spirit of the Bowl with which no one disagreed: the garden pergolas indicated that nature played an important role there, while the urns linked the origins of the Bowl's hillside amphitheater to classical Greece and ancient theatrical rituals.

The achievement of Carter's and Hertz's symphony series, however, set in motion a conflict between what might be described as "aural" and "visual" goals for those who directed performances at the Bowl. The desire to produce music in the immense space of the Bowl required a somewhat closed stage, whose frame would amplify sound and, perhaps more importantly, enable the musicians to hear one another. The desire to produce ballet, theater, and opera spectacles in the open demanded, conversely, a relatively unencumbered stage. This dilemma would determine the contours of the Bowl's architectural development throughout the 1920s.

Early struggle for control over programming and architectural improvements at the Bowl even resulted in the board's rejection in 1922 and 1923 of significant offers from William Andrews Clark, Jr., the founder of the Los Angeles Philharmonic, toward funding the construction of an amphitheater. Clark fashioned the Philharmonic into Los Angeles' first professional orchestra by underwriting a living wage for the Philharmonic's musicians nine months out of the year. The Bowl, he believed, was a perfect solution to the problem of providing summer income for his musicians. While Clark gave many substantial donations for the Bowl's operating budget and capital improvements, he made the largest of his offers contingent upon the board's raising specified amounts of money and agreeing to long-term contracts for the Philharmonic's players, which conditions the board could not accept.

Oil heiress Aline Barnsdall, who joined their group in 1923, was one of the most visible forces for the infusion of new music, theater, dance, architecture, and education into Los Angeles in the 1920s. It is not known how fully she participated in the physical development of the Bowl, but she made substantial donations that helped fund the 1923 season, retire the debt on the mortgage, and, in 1924, enable the commissioning of architectural and landscape plans. Indeed, during the four years that she served on the board, all the basic architectural elements that define the Bowl's performance arena today took shape. It is tempting to think that Barnsdall played a significant role, for she understood better than most the symbolic importance of an architectural frame for the Bowl's events. In 1919 she had commissioned the controversial American architect Frank Lloyd Wright to design his first Los Angeles work — a house and an arts complex on a 36-acre site in Hollywood that she named Olive Hill. Her "little principality," as Wright called it, included an amphitheater, and Wright's drawings and models for it reveal it as a precedent for the Bowl.

But, perhaps most consequential for the development of the Bowl's architecture, the board would commission Lloyd Wright, the architect's son who had worked on the Olive Hill project, to design orchestra shells for the seasons of 1927 and 1928. Lloyd Wright's contributions to the Bowl would establish it as a site for architectural innovation, just as the gifts of his patron Barnsdall brought music of such contemporary composers as Stravinsky and Ravel to its stage.

Barnsdall's donations could not carry the Bowl, however, and in 1924, the board made a decision that strengthened its financial future and ensured that it would become a cultural resource for the entire metropolitan area. This arrangement deeded the Bowl to Los Angeles County which would contribute funding for capital improvements and the operating budget and lease the Bowl back to the board for 99 years. At the end of the 1925 season, the County made $300,000 available for permanent improvements.

These were very good years for public building in Los Angeles, since the city was feeling the effects of the biggest boom in its history. It was the fastest growing city in the nation and the fifth largest by 1930. Downtown, the towered library designed by the New York architect Bertram Goodhue was near completion, and plans for a civic center were underway. Among the groups who promoted public architecture in Los Angeles was the Allied Architects, a cooperative society of 33 who formed an association in 1921 to pressure authorities to hire local architects. The Allied Architects had submitted plans for a civic center in 1924, and they succeeded in obtaining the County commission for work on the Bowl in 1926.

Pasadena architect Myron Hunt (1868-1952) together with the firm of Robertson and Bergstrom were the architects of record for the set of drawings that the Allied Architects submitted to the Bowl Association in February of 1926. Hunt's Pasadena Public Library (1924) and many of his residences are landmarks in Southern California, but two other works prepared him for his remarkable contributions to the Bowl: his preservation activities in the development of Pasadena's Arroyo Seco Park (from 1917) and his planning for the Rose Bowl (after 1919). Carrying forward the Rose Bowl experiments, Hunt's design for the Hollywood Bowl utilized a similar elliptical shape for the amphitheater that rose up from the orchestra pit. Monumental stairways embraced the amphitheater's circumference and reinforced the dynamics of its shape. Hunt's system of terraces, sections, and promenades, as well as the steel and concrete substructures containing dressing rooms and storage areas under the stage, is his enduring legacy at the Bowl. The inspiring form of his amphitheater is best seen from Mulholland Drive above the Bowl's northerly rim, where the "balloon" shape seems poised to fill with music and ascend. To provide shelter for concerts, Hunt suggested a rectilinear pavilion draped with cloth that could be easily dismounted. This removable structure, which had support buildings to either side, would have allowed for the extension of what he described as an open "verdure" stage far up into the hills opposite the amphitheater.

The new amphitheater opened in June 1926, with two spectacular extravaganzas that made excellent use of Hunt's desire to incorporate landscape into theatrical production: Charles Cadman's "Indian Opera" *Shanewis* and Nikolai Rimsky-Korsakov's symphonic suite for orchestra, *Scheherazade*. For *Shanewis*, teepees and campfires created an encampment in the hills opposite the amphitheater, and 200 Native Americans (sponsored by the U.S. Department of the Interior) joined a processional that moved one-quarter mile down the hillside to arrive at a powwow on the stage; for *Scheherazade*, a "castle" was constructed on the crest of the ridge, 75 feet above the stage, and the Shah made a slow, dramatic descent on a prancing white Arabian horse. But the symphony season demanded a protective covering over the stage for the orchestra, and in July 1926 a new structure took shape. Hunt's vision of a verdure stage slowly faded from prominence at the Bowl, and now, at the end of the 20th century, it seems as historically remote as the passion for pageantry, which it was designed to nourish.

The search for the architectural form of the Bowl's music shell was more complicated than that of the amphitheater and stage, perhaps because all concerned recognized that the shell would become the symbol of the enterprise. Between 1926 and 1929, four different music shells were designed and built for the Bowl, and their sequence tells a fascinating story of rivalry and disappointment. The Allied Architects' 1926 curvilinear music shell was the Bowl's first arched proscenium. Its wood frame had five walls that rose to meet the arch in curved sections. Its front consisted of two arches of different shapes: an elliptical arch to keep the structure low, so as not to hinder the view of the hills behind, and, inside the ellipse, a circular arch to frame the musicians. Covering the shell's face and inside back wall were illusionistic sea and landscape paintings with a strong flavor of the Orient, perhaps influenced by Meyer & Holler's architectural plans for Grauman's Chinese Theater in Hollywood (published in 1925). It foreshadowed the time when musicians' needs would take precedence over the directors' desires to expand their productions into the landscape.

Ironically, the Bowl's new shell, amphitheater, and site improvements, which were proud emblems of its rise as a cultural institution, played havoc with acoustics. The concave shell focused

Allied Architects submitted this sketch of a Myron Hunt design for improvements in 1926.

The 1926 construction was carried out by Herbert M. Baruch Corp.

sound from the stage to the center of the seats, where it reverberated unpleasantly against the newly-poured concrete surfaces of section dividers. A major landscape planting campaign was hurriedly undertaken in an attempt to correct the problem, but all concerned realized that progress was in many ways inimical to the Bowl's natural advantages.

The first architect to propose radical solutions for the functional, acoustical, and symbolic requirements of a music shell for the Bowl was Lloyd Wright, who designed shells for the Bowl's 1927

Lloyd Wright's design for the 1926 production of *Julius Caesar* made use of the entire canyon, accenting it with temples, bridges, and aqueducts.

The Hollywood Bowl

and 1928 seasons. Wright's shells were powerful statements of modern design as well as ground-breaking experiments in acoustics and illumination. The oldest son of Frank Lloyd Wright, Lloyd had trained with his father in Oak Park, Illinois, and later specialized in landscape architecture with the Olmsted firm (America's most prominent landscape architects) in Boston. He moved to San Diego in 1911 to work for the Olmsteds and, later, Irving Gill. In 1915, he opened a landscape architecture practice with Paul Thiene in Los Angeles, but he quickly turned his attention to set design for films and took a position as head of Paramount's art department in 1917. Although he was with Paramount less than two years, that experience, as well as his association during the 1920s with film and theater designers Norman Bel Geddes and Cedric Gibbons, would prove crucial for his work at the Bowl.

In 1926, in conjunction with the Allied Architects' extensive improvements, Wright prepared studies for general landscaping at the Bowl and an entrance drive. His plans were not implemented, but he was asked to design the sets for the closing production of the season, Gordon Craig's *Julius Caesar*. Wright made brilliant use of the empty verdure stage, accenting the landscape with triumphal Roman temples, bridges, and aqueducts. The effect of the *Julius Caesar* sets was stunning, and Wright went on to design the sets for the Bowl's 1927 opening production of Reginald De Koven's operetta *Robin Hood*. Wright's romantic evocations of the medieval Nottingham market place and sheltering thickets of Sherwood Forest seemed to grow almost naturally out of the canyon terrain, but again the

Lloyd Wright's 1927 shell under construction.

Lloyd Wright's pyramidal shell (1927) as seen from the top of the Bowl's amphitheater; at both sides of the stage apron are trees and other remnants of Wright's *Robin Hood* set.

returning symphony orchestra required a shell. This time Wright gained the commission and turned his creativity to finding an architectural solution that would mediate the competing needs of the Philharmonic programs and the theatrical spectaculars that opened and closed each season.

Legend has it that the commission came to Wright at the last minute and that wood left over from the dismantled *Robin Hood* sets was donated for his construction. Regardless of when or how Wright got the job, his shell was a masterpiece. He evolved the shell's pyramidal shape from inclined wall planes, which acted as sound reflectors. He allowed the diagonal braces in the lateral walls to act as "sound-trap louvers," and he placed horizontal light trays above the orchestra to provide soft, indirect lighting. While contemporary critics referred to the shape of Wright's shell as a teepee, its weight and density suggest much more forcefully the battered adobe and stone construction of the Mayans in Central America and the Pueblo Indians in North America. Wright himself declared its image to be that of the American Southwest. He searched, as had his father, for a design that would incorporate the indigenous roots of America's cultural heritage. His first instinct at the Bowl was to bring the idea of the Greek amphitheater closer to the American past.

Whatever the historical and formal inspirations of Wright's shell, some felt that it succeeded because it returned the Bowl — if only symbolically — to a more natural state. Bruno David Ussher, a music critic and, from 1935, the production manager at the Bowl, wrote that the neutral colors of Wright's shell complemented the brown, gray, and olive of the hills: "Somehow the Bowl has taken on something of its former oldness. Last year's improvements of the gardener and cement and landscape contractor jarred with newness." He also reported, however, that some Bowl patrons were upset by the shell and "expressed surprise and worse at the set." It was perhaps the primitive aspects of the shell that made some people uneasy with its form. Wright's shell of 1927 was, of course, built as a temporary structure, but it was a controversial idea doomed to appear only once.

If differences in taste doomed Wright's 1927 shell, his acoustical accomplishments may have saved his relationship with the Bowl's board, who commissioned him to design a second, more permanent shell for the 1928 season. They made a pointed request, however, for a circular music shell. The request must have had aesthetic rather than acoustic motivations since curvilinear forms tend to focus sound in the center of the audience. Wright complained cryptically that he could not understand "why a straight line is modern and a curved line not modern" and he took revenge on his critics, intentionally or not, by designing a sleek, curved Moderne shell that was every inch as provocative a contemporary shape as had been his Mayan pyramid. Wright labored diligently to devise a shape that would provide both musicians and concertgoers with excellent acoustical conditions. The architectural prototype on which he undoubtedly drew was the famous Auditorium Theater of Chicago (1889) — a building his father greatly admired — designed by Dankmar Adler and Louis Sullivan, in whose office the elder Wright had trained. Lloyd Wright's 1928 shell, however, was not only a startlingly modern form but also a new structural concept.

Wright formed the shell of nine concentric, segmental arches, which he shaped according to a "reflected ray" model of sound transmission. He made myriad calculations of the paths of sound from various instrumental groups to determine the dimensions and arcs of the shell's ring sections, as well as the height of the low wall that backed the orchestra. But it was also Wright's ingenious method of wood construction that made this shell a hallmark of 20th-century design. The shell differed from all of its progenitors in one essential way: it was a light-weight, prefabricated form of standard parts that could not only be rapidly assembled and

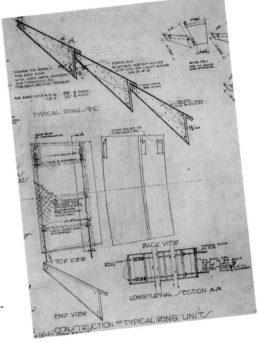

Detail of a construction drawing (1928) by Lloyd Wright showing a typical ring unit and turnbuckle system for "tuning" his curvilinear shell.

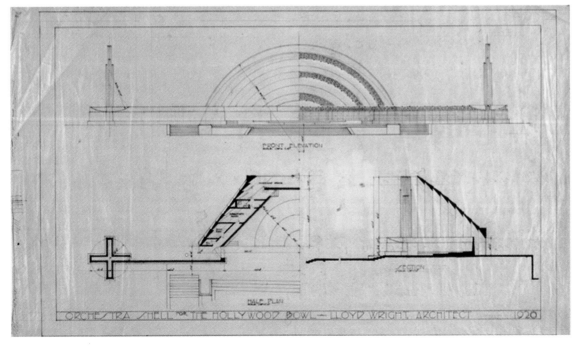

Preliminary drawing (1928) by Lloyd Wright for a curvilinear shell to replace his pyramidal shell of 1927.

Above: Wright's elliptical shell was immediately recognized as a modern classic.

Right: Night-time performance (1928).

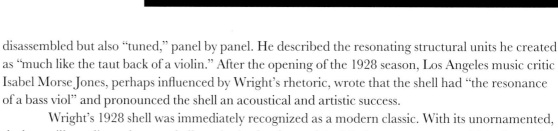

disassembled but also "tuned," panel by panel. He described the resonating structural units he created as "much like the taut back of a violin." After the opening of the 1928 season, Los Angeles music critic Isabel Morse Jones, perhaps influenced by Wright's rhetoric, wrote that the shell had "the resonance of a bass viol" and pronounced the shell an acoustical and artistic success.

Wright's 1928 shell was immediately recognized as a modern classic. With its unornamented, sleek curvilinear lines, the new shell was in the forefront of the Moderne movement, which changed the world of design in the late 1920s. The rapidity with which Moderne stylistic currents swept American theater, film, architecture, and the decorative and industrial arts is astonishing. Clearly Wright's shell was closely connected to events in the film industry in Hollywood, which played an important role in the popularization of the image that he created.

The influence of Wright's Moderne forms was seen almost immediately in Los Angeles' architecture. The Pelliser Building and Wiltern Theater (Morgan, Walls, and Clements, 1931) and the Los Angeles Times Building (Gordon Kaufmann, 1935) are perhaps the best-known examples. In addition, several of Busby Berkeley's classic Hollywood film sets, designed after 1930 for MGM and Warners, are close in spirit and form to Wright's ideas. The influence of these ideas was not limited to Los Angeles: his 1928 shell had effect throughout the country, most notably in New York in Joseph Urban's design for the auditorium of the New School for Social Research (1930) and in Radio City Music Hall (1932), whose design consultant "Roxy" (Samuel Lionel Rothafel) claimed that he got the inspiration for the hall in 1928 while watching a sunrise at sea.

Like its forerunner, Wright's second shell must have antagonized some members of the Bowl's board. Wright claimed his shell of 1928 characterized "the very essence of the democratic spirit that begot the Bowl... to distribute the great works of man to the many" but his arguments in defense of its image and acoustical accomplishments fell on deaf ears. Wright intended that it would be dismantled at the end of each summer symphony season so that performances requiring special sets could transform the stage and make use of the hillside behind it. For reasons that are today obscure, the shell was left standing through the winter of 1928, and it began to weather. As often happens when a building has enemies, its structural safety was called into question. Wright defended the shell's soundness and protested that it could be left to the elements and then tightened, relined, and repainted in one operation in the spring. However, in December 1928, Oliver G. Bowen, an engineer retained by the Bowl's board, recommended that the shell be demolished. The board authorized an attempt to reinforce it, but judged the work unsuccessful and voted for demolition in 1929.

The board then entrusted the design of the new shell to the engineering firm of Elliott, Bowen, and Walz, calling in physicist Vern O. Knudsen (who became a board member in the early 1960s) as an acoustical consultant. The Allied Architects constructed the shell for about $33,000 (Wright's 1928 shell had cost about $8,000). Their results created a dilemma: the form was popular and sturdy, but its acoustics were debatable. A semi-circle was substituted for Wright's ellipse, and transite (a mixture of cement and asbestos) was used instead of wood. Mounted on rails, the shell was removable but weighed 55 tons. It got the sound out into the amphitheater but, unfortunately, focused it. And it was particularly disadvantageous for the musicians, since it had no low interior walls to reflect sound and allow them to hear one another. Its portability proved questionable too; its weight soon crushed the wheels on which it was to roll, so that they had to be replaced, and later it derailed during a stage-change. Still in place, it has not been moved since the late 1960s. At the opening of the 1929 season, Isabel Jones assessed it: "[The new shell has] a harmonica tone due to the materials.... The upper seats in the center are best, but there is a loss of tone for seats in front. Perfection has, from a musical standpoint, been pushed further away than before." It was a conservative version of Wright's composition but over the decades it has become the Bowl's logo, its beloved icon.

If the "shell game" at the Bowl during the late 1920s had winners and losers, those oppositions softened with the passage of time. The Allied Architects, after all, preserved the visual essence of Wright's idea — telescoping concentric rings, which created a megaphone-shaped form. Indeed, in

The pool fountain, installed in 1959, played in rainbow hues at intermission.

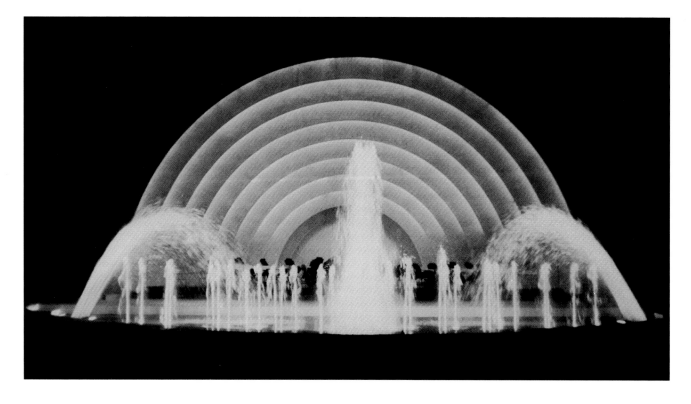

the 1970s, when Los Angeles architect Frank Gehry suggested replacing their shell with a rectangular open truss and, in effect, going back to the future, Wright defended the 1929 circular shell as if it were his own design.

Secure in the Bowl's solvency and growing international reputation, the board decided to augment its civic presence in the late 1930s with a heroic fountain that would stand as a gateway to the arena at the corner of Highland Avenue and the planned freeway. In 1938, Bowl president Charles Toberman (he served one term in 1923 and later, from 1934 to 1950) successfully petitioned the Works Progress Administration for public funds to build not only the fountain but a tearoom and restrooms as well. Sculptor George Stanley, most noted for his design of the Oscar statuette, designed a three-figure group — the Muses of Music, Drama, and Dance — which thematically captured the Bowl's inclusive spirit and performance history.

This fountain stands then, in part, as Toberman's legacy, for his was one of the clearest and steadiest voices for varied programming in the Bowl, a stance that he believed embodied the ideals of the Bowl's founders. Hollywood's foremost real estate developer, including such landmarks as Grauman's Egyptian Theater (1922), the Hollywood Roosevelt Hotel (1927), and Grauman's Chinese Theater (1927), Toberman charted a course to preserve the Bowl's natural environment and acoustical properties. In 1924 he negotiated to route Mulholland Drive so that its traffic would not be seen or heard from the Bowl. In 1929 he donated a strip of land from his Outpost holdings along the rim of the Bowl to insure that buildings would not encroach on the amphitheater. And he fought a battle to lower the bed of the Hollywood Freeway (completed in 1953) below grade to trap the noise and lights of the passing cars. Toberman lost, however, and this most serious assault on the Bowl's acoustics went forward, creating problems with which every architect and acoustician who works there must now contend.

Indeed, the construction of the Hollywood Freeway marked a low point in the history of the Bowl; following the war years when County authorities limited attendance (5,000 in 1942 and 10,000 in 1943) a downward spiral ensued. The Bowl closed suddenly and unexpectedly in July 1951, just after the season had opened. Dorothy Buffum Chandler immediately came to its rescue. Although the downtown Music Center would be Chandler's major architectural contribution to Los Angeles, her years on the Bowl's board in the 1950s gave the Bowl new life and focus. She appointed a blue-ribbon committee to prepare an extensive study of its operations, and upon the study's completion in 1952, the Bowl was rejuvenated by a series of facelifts. A reflecting pool in front of the stage was constructed in 1953 and sound towers were added in 1954. The industrial designer Henry Dreyfus (who became a board member in 1954) installed a fountain in the pool that played in rainbow hues at intermission. Dedicated in 1959 to Chandler, the fountain became a major attraction of the Bowl. The pool gave way to additional boxes in 1972.

One of the most important changes in the Chandler years, however, was the initiation of the custom of picnicking at the Bowl. With Chandler's backing, the removal of the "No Food" signs and the inauguration of contests for decorated picnic baskets encouraged the audience to participate in a pre-performance ritual of their own making. This custom has become so much a part of the Bowl experience that it has influenced a wide range of decisions about improvements there ever since.

The 1969 appointment of Ernest Fleischmann as executive director of the Los Angeles Philharmonic and general director of the Hollywood Bowl opened another period in its architectural evolution. Fleischmann, who demonstrated a genius for innovative programming, also had an evangelical drive to reach and excite new audiences with the power of classical music. To that end, he passionately pursued music and performers who were ideally suited for outdoor performance. His experiments demanded new sound and stage sets. Impressed with Frank Gehry's Merriweather Post

Architect Frank Gehry and acoustician Christopher Jaffe devised this Sonotube arrangement for the 1970 season.

Pavilion of Music (Maryland, 1967), Fleischmann asked the avant-garde Los Angeles architect to prepare plans for the Bowl's 1970 season. As a quick, inexpensive, and temporary solution, Gehry and acoustician Christopher Jaffe devised Sonotubes, which were manufactured cardboard forms for concrete columns. This solution improved ensemble conditions for the orchestra, but it was also a brilliant design concept that brought together ideas explored in earlier shells for the Bowl.

Then in 1980, also under Fleischmann's direction, Gehry created the fiberglass spheres that presently hang from the shell to reflect and distribute sound to the orchestra. Their acoustical effect is complemented by 150 loudspeakers distributed throughout the amphitheater. The image of Gehry's spheres has been described as the "effervescence [of an] architectural champagne cocktail." He carefully calculated their size and position within the canopy to unite auditory and visual perception in a playful game: the music seems to propel the spheres in a trajectory toward the audience and, at the same time, to push them toward the depths of the shell and even out into the canyon beyond. Thus Gehry regained the spatial abundance of the Bowl's site, which has been threatened since its founding.

As early as 1971, under Fleischmann's patronage and with the support of County Supervisor Kenneth Hahn, Gehry proposed a master plan for the site and a permanent — but revolutionary — solution for the perennial problem of the shell. He envisioned replacing the Allied Architects' shell with a large trussed frame that would have given greater presence to the stage from the back of the amphitheater and more versatility to the design of sets, which could have been hung from the truss. Gehry's project was not realized, but during the 1984 Olympics he offered Bowl audiences a taste of the possibilities that his truss would have opened. In collaboration with Ronald Hays and artist Peter Alexander, he hung a temporary scrim across the face of the shell and projected upon it abstract colorscapes.

In 1995, the most significant architectural interventions at the Bowl since Gehry's adaptation of the shell were underway. Because they did not include changes to the appearance of the shell itself, that landmark structure remains as one of the most widely circulated and recognizable symbols of the cultural life of Los Angeles. These improvements leave practically no existing building on the site other than the shell untouched. They enhance the technical infrastructure of the site — replacing

Gehry in collaboration with Ronald Hays and artist Peter Alexander hung a scrim with projected colorscapes for the 1984 Olympics.

Architects' model (1994) of the Hollywood Bowl Museum showing its relationship to Frank Gehry's open-air dining pavilion (on the right), which was built in 1981.

electrical, plumbing, and other utilities — but also begin to make a graceful group of the motley assortment of auxiliary structures that have been added over the years without the benefit of a master plan.

The Los Angeles office of Skidmore, Owings, and Merrill, an architectural firm headquartered in New York, in partnership with Kennard Design Group, won the bidding process for this multi-phased commission in 1993. Their scheme protects the Bowl's park-like nature by creating buildings that take on the character of their hillside in massing and selection of materials while achieving the primary goal of increasing services to the public. An enlarged Hollywood Bowl Museum will take its place on Peppertree Lane next to the open-air dining pavilion which Frank Gehry designed in 1981.

At this point in the Bowl's eight-decade history, it is appropriate that the new and expanded museum building be the first to greet visitors. Since 1984 the Bowl Museum has been one of the only venues in Los Angeles where the cultural history of the city has been consistently exhibited. The new building will more than double the gallery space. Five-term Los Angeles County Supervisor Edmund Edelman was — with Ernest Fleischmann — the driving force behind the establishment of the first Bowl Museum. Before retiring from the Board of Supervisors, Edelman saw through the $25.5 million bond issue which made possible the current building project. Edelman's vision and sponsorship demonstrate how much the Bowl's lasting vitality as a public performance arena and historic site depends upon enlightened political leadership in support of the arts.

The Bowl's historic shell will likely become the target of subsequent renovation, since its acoustical properties are not ideal for the seats closest to the stage and the ability of the musicians on the stage to hear one another. Any future consideration about the shape of the shell will surely take into account the creative thought that has been focused on its forms for three-quarters of a century. The Bowl's shell has been, is, and will continue to be the symbol of an enterprise which is communal in the most inspiring and hopeful visions of the role of the performing arts in city life.

How the Bowl Danced: An Era of Exploration

In its first two decades, the Hollywood Bowl helped make dance a vibrant 20th-century art form in Los Angeles and, in doing so, made it possible for many of the most important choreographers and performers to test their wings. Agnes de Mille, in *Dance to the Piper*, wrote of her 1935 commission for the Bowl. She was to receive $2,000 — an amount that had to cover two months of rehearsal, costumes for 80 performers, and her own creative time. When asked why she had accepted a job which would leave her with a deficit, she said, "It's an opportunity to compose works I've always longed to do."

From 1922 through 1940, the Hollywood Bowl was a special place for dance, and audiences, as well as critics, saw this art form making history, with attendance high and much press coverage. During this period, choreographers in Los Angeles had opportunities to experiment and explore on the huge stage, though often under severe financial constraints. They created new dances in the Hollywood Bowl, from an evocation of the evils of war to an erotic celebration of spring's awakening. Dancers performed with a variety of artists and in many styles, one night perhaps in toe shoes and the next in bare feet.

When the Bowl opened in 1922, dance in America was still in its early stages as an art form. There were those who, in the tradition of Isadora Duncan, were rejecting ballet's restrictions and searching for freer and more expressive forms of movement. Others were trying to establish standards and artistic possibilities for ballet and working to make it part of the American dance experience. Dance pioneers came to Los Angeles and saw it as a utopian place to teach, create, and try out their new ideas. By providing a prestigious venue for choreographers and dancers, the Hollywood Bowl became an active partner in allowing American dance to develop and mature.

At the Hollywood Bowl, the story of dance through the 1930s tells of the ways diverse artists were creating in Los Angeles and how they helped shape American dance. After 1940 a variety of circumstances combined to change the Bowl from a place showcasing original work on a regular basis to a stage that featured an occasional touring company.

Etenraku, 1937.

It all began with the arrival in Los Angeles of Ruth St. Denis, Ted Shawn, Norma Gould, and Ernest Belcher. These four were American dance pioneers, opening schools and creating performing groups that would encompass their vision of dance as a serious art form with high standards and new ideas. They earned the community's respect, and students flocked to their classes. It is interesting to note that their arrival coincided with two events, both related to growth in Los Angeles: D.W. Griffith directed his landmark film *The Birth of a Nation* in 1915; in that same year the Lusitania sank and the impact of World War I on Europe's film industry began to put Hollywood on the international map.

Ernest Belcher was the first dancer to be involved with the Bowl when he staged dances for a preseason presentation of *Carmen* on July 8, 1922, a prelude to the official opening July 11. He used 100 dancers and in the July 9th *Los Angeles Times* report of the evening, the reviewer wrote: "One of the prime attractions was the ballet, which not only visualized the dance numbers of *Carmen* itself, but also interpreted the fascinating *L'Arlésienne* Suite."

Marge Champion with her father Ernest Belcher, 1934.

The most remarkable thing about Belcher's 1922 work at the Bowl was that it allowed thousands of people, probably most for the first time, to see serious dance in the form of ballet. The only other ballet performances in Los Angeles around that time took place at Philharmonic Auditorium in the form of brief visits in 1921 by Russian stars Anna Pavlova and Adolph Bolm with their groups. Belcher's dancers at the Bowl were his students and over the years many of them became famous. They included Maria Tallchief (the great Balanchine ballerina, who would return to the Bowl with the Ballet Russe de Monte Carlo in the 1940s), actress/dancers Gwen Verdon, Cyd Charisse, Nanette Fabray, and Rita Hayworth, and Belcher's own daughter Marge Champion and her husband Gower Champion.

During the next twelve years, Belcher created nine evenings of dance for the Bowl. The most spectacular of these was his 1932 evening-long ballet *Elysia*, commissioned as a tribute to the Olympic Games held in Los Angeles that year.

During this time Belcher also worked as dance director on over 200 movies, including *Salome vs Shenandoah*, *The Phantom of the Opera*, *The Jazz Singer*, *Anna Karenina*, and *The Little Princess*. Shirley Temple, Pola Negri, Ramon Novarro, and Colleen Moore were among the many movie stars who studied with him. In 1931 Cecil B. De Mille built him a three-story studio of 36,000 square feet and Belcher had well over 2,000 students, men and women who came to him for serious and disciplined study.

The Hollywood Bowl audience was treated to an entirely different sort of dance when Ruth St. Denis and Ted Shawn performed there in 1927. With Alfred Hertz conducting music of Liszt, Delibes, and Glazunov, they danced two solos and a duet, filling the vast stage with charismatic performances and strong visual imagery. Not for them Belcher's more traditional definition of virtuosity, with its rapid and numerous turns, spectacular backbends and leaps, and extensive work in beribboned toe shoes. St. Denis and Shawn did a good portion of their dancing in bare feet, and emphasized movements of hands, torso, and head instead of the leg and footwork typical of ballet.

Known internationally as artists searching for dance forms that were expressive and spiritual, these two had chosen Los Angeles as the starting point for their collaboration when they founded the Denishawn School in 1915. This became one of the most important early schools in American dance, known for stimulating performance and creativity in new realms of movement. Martha Graham, Doris Humphrey, and Charles Weidman, recognized as innovators of 20th-century American dance, were students at the Los Angeles Denishawn School, as were such movie stars as Louise Brooks, Ruth

Chatterton, and Ina Claire. Although they did include ballet in their school curriculum, St. Denis and Shawn wanted to break away from what they perceived as its rigid vocabulary and formal structure. They emphasized finding ways to explore movement that expressed the inner being, utilizing yoga, various ethnic forms, and the system of dramatic gesture and plastiques based on theories of François Delsarte.

The appearance of Ruth St. Denis and Ted Shawn at the Bowl came a few months after a Denishawn Company tour of the Orient from September 1925 through November 1926. It was the first time an American dance group made such a tour. In 1922 Shawn and St. Denis had left their Los Angeles school in the hands of experienced former students and by 1927 were in the midst of building a Denishawn House in New York City. Their Bowl performance came just before the two

Norma Gould Dancers, 1929.

Norma Gould, 1929.

artists began to go their own ways, and as former students, including Martha Graham, began to come forward with bold new ideas, eventually to take leadership in contemporary American dance.

Norma Gould was the last of the four pioneers to bring her artistry and imagination to the Hollywood Bowl stage. Her first two performances, in 1927 and 1928, were post-season evenings called "California Night of Music." The printed program gives no details about the 1927 choreography, but we know she was accompanied in 1928 by Adolph Tandler's Little Symphony in the premiere of her new ballet, *The Shepherd of Shiraz*. The story was by Alice Pike Barney and the music by Sigurd Frederickson.

In 1929 Gould was asked to prepare an evening of dance for the regular season, on August 30. The orchestra was conducted by Sylvain Noack, the concertmaster of the Los Angeles Philharmonic, and the program consisted of two dances which Gould created especially for the Bowl stage. The first, *Unfinished Symphony*, was set to Schubert's eponymous B-minor Symphony. The other was set to Tchaikovsky's *Nutcracker* Suite. In 1929, audiences were not yet besieged by a plethora of Christmas performances of *Nutcracker*.

Bertha McCord Knisely, in a *Los Angeles Saturday Night* article dated September 7, 1929, reported on Gould's performance at the Hollywood Bowl. She noted the *Unfinished Symphony* had "a dignified, serious conception of humanity's vacillation between faith and doubt." Pictures of the dancers suggest an emphasis on grouping and plastique, as opposed to complex steps and athletic virtuosity.

Norma Gould was born in Los Angeles and began teaching dance after graduating from high school in 1908. Ted Shawn came to Los Angeles in 1911, after initial ballet studies in Denver, and soon started working with Gould. Both young artists were interested in developing ideas beyond classical ballet and decided that working as a ballroom team would finance other creative work. They danced for tango teas at the Angelus and Alexandria Hotels; other activities included a short 1913 film on the history of dance for the Edison Company, and a two-week engagement at San Diego's Mirror Theater, later known as the Majestic.

In 1914 Gould and Shawn embarked for New York on the Sante Fe Railroad, having been hired as entertainers to perform at employee recreation centers along its line. But in New York they went their separate ways. Shawn met Ruth St. Denis, and they became not only husband and wife, but also dancing partners. Gould returned to Los Angeles. She resumed teaching and performing, and came under the management of Los Angeles impresario L.E. Behymer. In a letter to her he wrote: "I have watched in the press your recent success and am doubly your admirer for the standard you have set and what you are doing to help elevate, entertain, and particularly add to the artistic influences of this city."

Norma Gould created her Dance Theater in 1932, at 118 Larchmont Boulevard in Los Angeles. Dance Theater was an umbrella unit for a wide array of performances which was to have positive repercussions for Los Angeles dance. Gould became an impresario, using her studio as a place for artistic exchange and a performance space for young artists struggling to make their own statement. In 1935 she moved her studio and Dance Theater to 831 South La Brea and through 1941 continued presenting artists such as Carmelita Maracci, Lester Horton, Tom Youngplant and Hopi Indians, Prince Modupe and the Nigerian Ballet, and many others.

In 1927 *The American Dancer* magazine was founded in Los Angeles; in 1929 Michel Fokine and Anna Pavlova were quoted as saying they would open schools in the city, although that never happened. Nonetheless, in 1929 a *Los Angeles Times* headline read: "L.A. Takes Lead as Dance Center," and by the 1930s there were thousands of dancers in Los Angeles. The 1929 depression did not affect the movie industry to any large degree. Nowhere else could dancers be employed during those years with such good and steady salaries and cheap housing.

Dance at the Hollywood Bowl reflected this surge in available talent. The 1922 makeshift stage was eliminated, a formal stage was built and large audiences could be accommodated (although most attendance estimates for the early decades at the Bowl are generous and highly imprecise). In *Dance to the Piper*, Agnes de Mille gave a clear impression of the challenges that the Bowl presented for a choreographer in 1935:

"The Bowl can seat about 19,000 people. The distance from the rear rows to the stage was so great that a gesture was perceptible a beat ahead of the sound. The Bowl stage was then in front of the orchestra shell and stretched to 104 feet in width. The arc of radiation being acres wide, there seemed to be no center and no sides. Where most stages fronted three sections of seats, this monster faced twelve. One's head moved 180 degrees to take in the front row. All patterns flattened right out, unaccented and unfocused like a panoramic photograph. Everything subtle or delicate disappeared. The solo figure did not exist. It was quite a challenge to a soloist who in London had worked on a twelve-foot stage and made a name for delicate facial expressions."

But the Bowl also offered unique compensations for the challenges it posed, as De Mille discovered at her dress rehearsal. "The air was cool at night. I stretched out my arms in the moonlight and flew. I raced and raced in the cool night expanse, on the largest stage in the world. Around me the mountains ribbed the sky. Under my feet lay the beat of a full symphony orchestra."

Through 1933, in addition to Belcher, St. Denis, Shawn, and Gould, among those who had performances at the Bowl, often more than once, are: Maud Allan (1926); Pavley and Oukrainsky (1928); Fokine and Fokina (1929); Albertina Rasch (1930); Adolph Bolm (1931); José Fernández (1931); Theodore Kosloff (1932); Fanchon and Marco, and Aida Broadbent (1933); Harold Hecht (1933); and Benjamin Zemach (1933). Through 1940 many of these choreographers appeared again, in addition to performances by Kurt Baer von Weisslingen, Francesca Braggiotti, Maria Gambarelli, Agnes de Mille, Stowitts, Pearl Wheeler, Martha Deane and Robert Tyler Lee, Michio Ito, Lester Horton, and Bronislava Nijinska.

A significant number of these artists created original work for the Bowl, while others re-created dances they had done on other stages. Among the works created for the Hollywood Bowl during the 1930s, three represent important milestones in American dance: Adolph Bolm's *The Spirit of the Factory* (1931); Benjamin Zemach's *The Victory Ball* (1935); and Lester Horton's *Le sacre du printemps* (1937). Each of these ballets is an example of daring choreography in which the artists fully developed their ideas and created unusual evenings of dance.

Although it is the choreographers and their work that is best documented, for young dancers the Hollywood Bowl stage was an important training ground and shaping influence. Some dancers worked with only one choreographer, but most performed with at least two or three. This meant they were exposed to different styles, ideas, and demands and had rare opportunities for growth and development.

ADOLPH BOLM: The Spirit of the Factory (1931)

In April 1931, the management of the Hollywood Bowl announced that it had secured Adolph Bolm's services for an evening of dance that summer. Due to the choreographer's international prestige, there were more than the usual number of pre-performance reports and articles in newspapers. Born in Russia, Bolm was a member of the Imperial Ballet in St. Petersburg until he resigned in 1910 to join the famous Ballets Russes, headquartered in Paris. In 1917 he initiated an independent career in the United States. Bolm's best-known concert choreography before the Bowl venture was to Stravinsky's *Apollon musagète* in 1928, first given at the Library of Congress and predating the Balanchine-Stravinsky collaboration.

The ballet that premiered on July 28, 1931 at the Bowl, with Artur Rodzinski conducting, was set to a score, also known as *The Iron Foundry*, by Alexander Mossolov. It was a futuristic work, with striking costumes and music that clanged, scraped, and hissed. Bolm's dancers moved with harshness and angularity to show the dehumanization imposed by society's new and omnipresent technology.

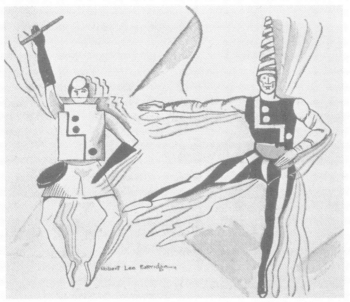

Costume study and performance of *The Spirit of the Factory*, 1931.

Bolm had originally conceived the ballet for a movie on which he had worked called *The Mad Genius* with John Barrymore. According to a May 1931 article in *Theatre Arts Monthly*, Bolm was hired to be "technical director, advisor, and ballet master of a film... dealing with the life of a Russian ballet impresario." Only a few fragments of Bolm's ballet were used in the movie.

Photographs of *The Spirit of the Factory* clearly show various aspects of Bolm's inventive ballet — bold groupings, expressive torsos, and defined movement. Cyril W. Beaumont, in *The Complete Book of Ballets*, noted that the ballet opened "with a blast on a steam siren which is the signal for the dancers representing various units of machinery to move... The groups continually change in accordance with the pounding rhythm of the music, each group a complete unit in itself, yet all contributing to present a tremendous spectacle of concerted rhythm." The work provokes thoughts about European art movements concerned with mechanization and machines — Italian and Russian futurists, Germany's Bauhaus style, and Russian constructivists. Bolm's work in Europe through 1917 would certainly have exposed him to these ideas.

The Spirit of the Factory was a huge success. "One might read numerous sociological protests into the choreography to account for its disturbing effect," Patterson Greene wrote in his review for the *Los Angeles Examiner*. "With or without these, it was a memorable artistic achievement — one that merits another showing."

It was performed twice more at the Hollywood Bowl: later in 1931 (with Pierre Monteux conducting) and also in 1932 (restaged for a larger company of 60 dancers). It was also chosen for the inaugural performance of the San Francisco Operatic and Ballet School in 1933 and repeated during the 1940 season of Ballet Theatre. Bolm had created a bold dance with a strong and contemporary message, and he received enthusiastic applause and approval from audience members and critics.

BENJAMIN ZEMACH: The Victory Ball (1935)

A ballet created for the Hollywood Bowl stage crying out against abuses of money, riches, and power? That is what Benjamin Zemach created in *The Victory Ball*, which had originally castigated not only the horrors and destruction wrought by wars, but also those for whom wars represented opportunities for financial gain. In the version Zemach originally rehearsed on the Hollywood Bowl stage, he included a scene correlating the enrichment of stockbrokers with war's destruction. For each act of war there was a corresponding act of profit, exemplified on stage by the addition of higher numbers to the riches accumulated by stockbrokers.

Zemach recalled in a 1989 conversation that the Bowl's management of the time had indicated that they had gotten more than they had bargained for. They had been agreeable to the anti-war theme, but were not pleased with a portrayal of the rich getting richer on war spoils.

The Victory Ball, 1935.

According to Zemach, "There was quite a hullabaloo about the stockbroker scene… and a stormy session with Mrs. Irish." He was referring to the formidable woman then in charge of the Bowl, Mrs. Leiland Atherton Irish.

In spite of the fact that Zemach had to eliminate this scene, the ballet was strong enough to make its message clear. Viola Hegyi Swisher's review in the *Hollywood Citizen News* of August 2, 1935 carried the headline: "Zemach's Tragic 'Victory Ball' Ballet Thrills Vast Bowl Throng: Horror of War Told in Dance." She felt the ballet was a great success: "Genius swept a fleeting hand across the Hollywood Bowl last night. A figurative tear and satire stirred bitterness there while a deeply impressed audience witnessed Benjamin Zemach's dance poem… Music, movement, color, lights all were fused into one powerful expression of protest against blood lust, bombast, shallowness, hypocrisy, greed — in short — War."

Zemach based his ballet on a poem by Alfred Noyes, and the music was by Ernest Schelling. The cast of characters for *The Victory Ball* included generals, diplomats, profiteers, dowagers, debutantes, soldiers, mothers, and death. Zemach did not want to interpret the words of the Noyes poem literally. He used them as a jumping-off point, while developing visual and sculptural sequences of movement to examine and demonstrate the brutality, despair, and disaster that come with war.

Designer Blandings Sloan created a projection on glass that filled the arch of the Hollywood Bowl with crosses. Swisher's review described the ballet thus:

"While the dancers whirled about in a gaily colored ballroom scene, silent shadows of war played an *obligato* across the Bowl shell. Fields fertile with dead men and marked by crosses, soldiers going over the top to infinity — these were silhouetted in the background while sub-debs and statesmen, smartly tailored officers and sleekly gowned women danced and flirted at the Victory Ball. Then came a war scene, leaving some of the dead and bereaved to make a chilling lacy pattern along the front of the stage…."

Born in Russia, Zemach received his early training there. His theater mentors were the experimental directors Constantin Stanislavsky, Yevgeny Vakhtangov, and Vsevelod Meyerhold; in dance he was trained by Russian teachers of Dalcroze Eurythmics, ballet, and modern dance.

The first contemporary theater utilizing spoken Hebrew, called Habima, was founded by Benjamin Zemach's brother Nahum in Moscow. From the very beginning, when rehearsals started in 1917, Benjamin was an active participant. The artistic freedom that had characterized the early years of the Russian revolution began to disappear in 1927; Benjamin and his brother left Russia for the United States, living first in New York and then in Los Angeles, where Nahum Zemach established a drama school (which he advertised in Hollywood Bowl programs). Benjamin Zemach created his first ballet for the Hollywood Bowl, *Fragments of Israel*, in 1933.

Among those influenced by Zemach in Los Angeles were Arnold Tamon, Robert Bell, Waldeen Falkenstein, Charles Ewing, Thelma Babitz (Genecin), and Frieda Flier (Maddow). Babitz and Flier went with Zemach to New York in 1936, when he was invited by Max Reinhardt to work on *The Eternal Road*; in 1937 both women were invited to become members of the Martha Graham Company. Frieda Flier Maddow spoke in 1986 of the lifelong impact Zemach had on her as an artist and dancer:

"Benjamin made you participate in the creative process; he made you feel you had something in you, that you had ideas… He gave meaning to dance. It was not just technique… Benjamin wanted to make sure that dance for us was not superficial, but it was a deeper, inner process."

LESTER HORTON: Le sacre du printemps (1937)

Lester Horton's Hollywood Bowl choreography to Igor Stravinsky's music marked the first time it was used by an American-born choreographer, and only the fourth time the score had been used for dance. The first choreography to the Stravinsky music was, of course, created by Vaslav Nijinsky in 1913 for the Paris season of the Ballet Russe. Léonide Massine staged two productions of *Le sacre du printemps*: 1920 in Paris and 1930 in New York at the Metropolitan Opera House with Martha Graham in the leading role.

Horton's work for the Hollywood Bowl featured Bella Lewitzky as The Chosen One and was quite different from the versions by Nijinsky and Massine. Here was ritual by an American from the

Igor Stravinsky.

Bella Lewitzky in rehearsal for
Le sacre du printemps, 1937.

perspective of the new Western frontier. Everything in the choreography spoke to the large expanses and freedom of the American West. Movement was broad, colors bright, energy high. The dance vocabulary was sensuous, erotic, weighted, and forceful. The theatricality was bold and clean, and lent an American impulse to the Russian sonorities and rhythms.

This was not a brooding ritual determined by stark contrasts of Russian winters and springs. This was a spring ritual celebrating a California landscape, where flowers bloomed all year and the sun was only intermittently broken with rain and mild cold. The energy of spring was not a sudden awakening but rather the continuation of a utopian environment's eternal promise.

Those who danced Horton's *Sacre* symbolized young people creating their own religion of action and adventure, promise and hope. The tight groupings of the Russian *Sacre* (both Massine's and Nijinsky's) were transformed into the large, open spatial patterns of Horton's *Sacre* — symbolizing a land where ritual had to do with new discoveries and unfathomed, open-ended landscapes. Horton's dancers moved with thrusting hips and aggressive arms and thighs, reaching out to the landscape. The muted colors and intricate designs of costumes used by the Russian choreographers were transformed into bright reds, yellows, and vibrant browns.

Lester Horton's choreography for *Le sacre du printemps* received enthusiastic reviews from the press and a somewhat hesitant reception from the audience. There was nothing traditionally pretty about this dance, and many in the audience did not know how to react.

Bella Lewitzky, who went on to become an internationally famous choreographer with her home base in Los Angeles, shared her memories in 1980. "Horton's *Sacre* was way ahead of its times. It had an Americanized feeling, and he emphasized the universality of ritual and celebration of the seasons. Audience reaction was violent, and controversy raged pro and con. I remember the pounding rhythms and a great deal of angularity. The dance opened with the 'Tribal Response to Spring,' with the groups beating upon the ground to waken it."

Members of the audience were not the only ones to have problems. William Bowne, who danced in the piece and worked with costuming, remembered in 1980 that the orchestra was reluctant to rehearse the score because of its difficulty and strangeness.

"Efrem Kurtz (conductor of the Ballet Russe de Monte Carlo) was supposed to conduct, but after rehearsing the orchestra once, he considered them inadequate to play the score and walked away, handing the baton over to the concertmaster. Horton received $1,000 for the performance but turned the money over to the orchestra so that he could have another rehearsal. As it was, the score was still too difficult and the finale was played in modified form."

The work took months of rehearsal and there were many costumes that had to be created. Even if he had not given his fee to the orchestra, Horton would still have been in debt.

Lester Horton was a relatively young choreographer, 29 years old, when he created this bold work to Stravinsky's music. He had arrived in Los Angeles in 1928 from his native Indianapolis and by 1932 was asked to be part of an Olympic Dance Festival at

Philharmonic Auditorium, where he showcased his young group of dancers and his choreography. In 1934 he presented a complete evening of his own work at the Shrine Auditorium and in the next three years gave frequent concerts at Norma Gould's Dance Theater, the Figueroa Playhouse, and Philharmonic Auditorium.

The commissioning of a Horton ballet by the Hollywood Bowl marked significant acceptance of his art by leaders of Los Angeles' cultural life. There, on a large stage, Horton emerged into the public eye. He created a work in which his style blossomed fully, in all its rich use of music and theatricality. Horton stayed in Los Angeles and developed into an artist whose work is now internationally recognized. In 1948 he opened his own Dance Theater. It was there that Bella Lewitzky, Alvin Ailey, Carmen de Lavallade, Joyce Trisler, James Truitte, designer Rudi Gernreich, and others had their own forum for expression and experimentalism. Lester Horton died in 1953; his friend, drama critic Frank Eng kept the Dance Theater going for seven years. However, by that time many of Horton's dancers had left to forge their own independent careers and carry on his legacy.

Dance at the Hollywood Bowl from 1922 through 1940 was characterized by exciting artistic exploration. Choreographers were encouraged to create, and dance was considered important on the Bowl stage. But conditions for performers and choreographers were never good. They received a flat amount, usually $1,000 to $2,000, covering expenses and fee. There were no contracts, which meant that rehearsal times on stage and with the orchestra were never spelled out, always to the detriment of the dancers.

After the orchestra rehearsed in the morning, dancers were offered the stage at noon and their feet would burn and blister from the heat. Agnes de Mille talks about her $2,000 fee and how she couldn't afford the two stage managers necessary to coordinate lighting and stage activity. As a result, during performance, the electrician did not turn the lights up after the first cue, leaving everything barely visible. It was not surprising that in 1937 The Dancers' Federation was organized, in the words of its materials, "to remove the appalling abuses which the dancers had been forced to suffer in the Hollywood Bowl."

By 1938 dancers in Los Angeles had gone one step further; they organized to form a permanent Hollywood Bowl Ballet. For a year it looked good but by 1939 it was clear that support was not forthcoming from wealthy individuals in Los Angeles or elsewhere. There were attempts to keep Los Angeles dance on the Bowl stage, and there were still some noteworthy events: Michio Ito's *Etenraku* (1937); the Albertina Rasch Ballet (1939); an evening of ballet by Bronislava Nijinska, who was then teaching and working in Los Angeles, featuring the U.S. premieres of works previously done in Europe (1940); and Adolph Bolm returned to Stravinsky in 1940, with new choreography for *Firebird* (the suite).

The wave of original dance presented at the Hollywood Bowl came to an end in 1941 when the touring company, Ballet Russe de Monte Carlo, appeared for three evenings. It was less expensive and easier to bring in a group that had its own organizational structure and funding.

During the years following the fertile '20s and '30s there was less dance at the Bowl, but the touring companies that did appear on the stage provided a mix of styles and represented some of the world's best dancing. Among the groups that have appeared since the 1940s are the Ballet Russe de Monte Carlo, Ballet Folklórico de México (in its U.S. debut), Martha Graham, the Bolshoi Ballet, the Royal Ballet (with Margot Fonteyn and Rudolf Nureyev), Antonio and the Ballet de Madrid, José Greco and His Spanish Dancers, Festival Polynesia, and members of the New York City Ballet led by Mikhail Baryshnikov and Peter Martins. Ballet was no longer a regular part of the Bowl schedule, but the dancing had not come to an end. On three evenings in July 1992, Julio Bocca and Eleonora Cassano joined John Mauceri and the Hollywood Bowl Orchestra for a dance program including scenes from *Swan Lake* (Petipa) and *Romeo and Juliet* (MacMillan), as well as Balanchine's complete *Who Cares?* (to music by Gershwin). The focus of dance at the Bowl may have shifted from original choreography to dancers, but those dancers were stars indeed!

Baryshnikov.

A HOME FOR OPERA

BY HERBERT GLASS

In the beginning, even before Alfred Hertz launched the first "Symphonies Under the Stars" concert on July 11, 1922, there was opera at the Bowl. Just three days earlier, on July 8, the naughty heroine of Bizet's *Carmen* kicked up her heels on a purpose-built stage in the Bowl.

The production was in the hands of a team headed by Alexander Bevani, "grand opera impressario [*sic*] from the East," to whom the Bowl was rented for a single performance, with the intended dual purpose of thrilling the multitudes and raising money to provide the facility with additional benches. From all reports, the performance — conducted by "the illustrious Maestro Cavaliere Fulgenzio Guerreri," — went well, but not without some massive blunders in the preparation, chronicled in infinite but usually sympathetic detail in the press which, like most of Los Angeles, was infected with Bowlmania.

Some confusion lay in the numbers: What on earth was the Bowl's capacity? It ranged from 20,000 to 40,000, depending on which authoritative spokesman (they were legion) you listened to and what you regarded as the legitimate boundaries of the amphitheater.

The more readily solved problems had to do with confusion over tickets. Many who had bought subscriptions to Symphonies Under the Stars saw *Carmen* ads announcing that "a full Philharmonic orchestra" would participate, followed next by a stern warning to subscribers that the Philharmonic was most emphatically *not* involved and that their tickets would not entitle them to see *Carmen*.

A few days before *Carmen*, the *Hollywood Daily Citizen* informed that the "Los Angeles Philharmonic Orchestra, led by Director William Henry Rothwell, has been engaged to play for the Opera." Rothwell, as it turned out, was vacationing in Europe at the time, while Hertz and the Philharmonic were busy rehearsing for their own opening.

Carmen enlisted as many as 500 performers — solo singers, choristers, instrumentalists, dancers — involved in what, according to impresario Bevani, would be "the first time an outdoor operatic spectacle of this sort has been produced since *Aida* was presented at the foot of the Pyramids 30 years ago."

Pavarotti rehearses.

It is doubtful that sufficient money was left to cover the production bills once the Bowl Association had taken its cut for the benches, doubts confirmed by the fact that two nights after the staged opera, the *Carmen* principals offered a "benefit concert," presumably for themselves, about which details are sketchy at best.

The *Los Angeles Times* review of *Carmen* by Edwin Schallert, the paper's drama (not music) critic — the most informative commentary among several which appeared in L.A.'s then very lively and numerous daily newspapers — is worth quoting at some length:

"Memories of old California midsummer fetes and festivals, when the click of castanets and the songs of Spain filled the orange-scented air were revived and idealized with the presentation of the grand opera *Carmen* last night at the Hollywood Bowl... It established the fitness of the Southland as the locale for open-air music. Even as the outdoor drama has come into its own domain in California, so will opera.

"Throngs upon throngs of people crowding... automobiles threaded their way up from Hollywood Boulevard to the hills long ere the announced hour of the performance. Throngs upon throngs reaching their objective gave themselves up to the spell of the melody and song, of enchanting rhythms and brilliant stage pictures, of dancing and drama and romance.

"Estimates place the attendance at the picturesque production at thirty thousand persons. From the stage, with its pyramid-like pillars, up into the distant hills stretched rows and rows of benches, filled with gazers and listeners. On the hills surrounding the amphitheater little groups of people clustered... Thousands to whom grand opera was a new and strange experience showed high anticipations...

"But with the first throbbing note of the Bizet music from the orchestra, there swept over the rows upon rows a commanding silence. All eyes were on the curtain which concealed the setting of the stage and its background of vague and ghostly hills and green. Then, with a fuller chord from the brass instruments, the curtain parted, and one saw tiled roofs and plastered dwellings, strangely akin to those relics of old days of Spain in California. Rapidly the setting filled with men clad in yellow and red uniforms and girls wearing bright shawl and mantilla.

"Opera in the outdoors is leagues separated from that which attracts the society patronage in the auditorium. A much broader audience is reached... Performances must have a greater sweep and greater force than those which are staged indoors."

Schallert further described the lavishness of the settings, the splendor of the dancing, the full-throatedness of the chorus, and gave high marks to a cast headed by Marguerita Sylva, only in her 20s but already an experienced Carmen on three continents; the Don José, Edward Johnson, who in 1935 would become managing director of New York's Metropolitan Opera; and one Henri Scott as Escamillo. He noted, too, that the local "Spanish community turned out in force, including many Angelenos of Castillian ancestry as members of the chorus, which was directed by Manuel Sanchez de Lara."

Carmen would become the Bowl's favorite opera, presented in staged or concert form, abbreviated or nominally complete, in no fewer than 11 seasons. After 1922, however, big-time opera was effectively cut off at the Cahuenga Pass for a time by financial realities. Outside presenters, aware of the losses sustained by Bevani, were unwilling to commit, and the Philharmonic had a hard enough time financing its orchestral concerts.

Which is not to say that *singers* were ever absent for long. As early as July 20 of the inaugural season, 1922, a local soprano, Constance Balfour, joined Hertz and the Philharmonic in a partially operatic evening "for the exclusive entertainment of visiting dentists." A dental convention had hired the orchestra for the occasion, the program being repeated in a public concert the following evening. A tradition was established by Balfour's singing of what would remain to this day the two arias most frequently performed in the Bowl: "Depuis le jour" from Charpentier's *Louise* and "The Prayer" — i.e., "Vissi d'arte" — from Puccini's *Tosca*.

WORLDS Greatest Production of CARMEN" IN HOLLYWOOD BOWL 7-8-22 © C.W. BEAM 1922 L.A. Photo.

Later during that first full summer, another local soprano, Mariska Aldrich, was quoted after an acoustical rehearsal for her concert with the Philharmonic: "It is a heavenly place to sing. Tonight, when I sing the *Tristan und Isolde* [the "Liebestod," another Bowl perennial-in-the-making], I shall begin it pianissimo, so that I can scarcely hear myself, and yet I am sure that the Bowl acoustics are so perfect that my voice will be carried to the topmost rim."

Another operatic non-event of note took place in 1923, when the Philharmonic attempted, without success, to engage Siegfried Wagner to conduct the music of his father, Richard, in the Bowl. But there was good news on August 3 when the amphitheater created its first star: baritone Lawrence Tibbett, son of a Bakersfield sheriff (shot to death by an outlaw he was pursuing) and a mother who ran a rooming house in Long Beach. Tibbett, making his professional debut, dazzled the crowd (including a scout from the Metropolitan Opera) with the *Pagliacci* Prologue (whose composer was listed in the house program as "Looncavallo") and the Toreador Song from *Carmen*. He was immediately re-engaged for later the same season, this time bringing "Wotan's Farewell" from *Die Walküre*.

During the following few summers there were still lots of arias, including those sung in a pre-season concert (then as now, "seasons" were preceded by "pre-seasons," "openings" by "pre-openings") on June 5, 1924, by Amelita Galli-Curci. The great Italian coloratura, according to chronicler Grace C. Koopal (*Miracle of Music*, 1972), set an "attendance record of 21,873 that has been exceeded only once in the history of the Bowl, by Lily Pons in 1956 with 26,410." (Schallert's estimated 30,000 for

the 1922 *Carmen* for some reason no longer counted.)

Not the rarities in symphony orchestras' winter seasons that they are today, singers of the operatic persuasion became staple ingredients of Bowl evenings. Regulars from the 1920s onward would include, in addition to Tibbett, such of his fellow crossover artists — singers, particularly the Americans, casually moved from the Met to the Bowl to radio and, later, to film, from Verdi one moment, to "The Road to Mandalay," "Because," or "Danny Boy" the next — as Richard Crooks, John Charles Thomas, Grace Moore (who would appear in the Bowl's first *Faust* in 1934 and often thereafter), Richard Bonelli (a durable local favorite), Nelson Eddy, Jan Kiepura (the Polish-born heartthrob), and Mario Lanza.

There were by 1929 potted Wagner operas in concert, not merely the programs of Wagner overtures and arias then so dear to audiences around the world. In that year, Eugene Goossens conducted 80-minute-long versions of *Tannhäuser* and *Walküre*. And during the same summer, again under Goossens, there was a concert *Carmen*. The new decade promised to be rich in operatic treasure.

The late-'20s and early-'30s, particularly with the film industry's presumed need for vocal instructors, also saw the Bowl and Los Angeles in general becoming a retreat for distinguished old-timers nearing careers' end, such as Elsa Alsen (Brünnhilde in the '29 *Walküre*) and Margarete Matzenauer, both of whom would establish vocal studios here; Maria Jeritza; the beloved American soprano Rosa Ponselle; and contralto Ernestine Schumann-Heink, surrogate mother to the countless British and American troops she entertained during World War I. Schumann-Heink had sung at a Bowl benefit during the "pre-opening" summer of 1921 and would return in triumph in 1928, one stop on what was neither her first nor last "official farewell tour." She would eventually end her days in Los Angeles.

Of that 1928 concert, the *Los Angeles Times*' Isabel Morse Jones wrote, "The biggest night in Bowl history! That incomparable conductor, Bernardino Molinari, and the most beloved of singers, Ernestine Schumann-Heink, drew into the Hollywood Bowl a crowd so large that it was impossible to estimate."

The most furiously promoted operatic event of the '20s was another pre-season presentation, the West Coast premiere of *Shanewis*, a one-acter by the American "Indianist" Charles Wakefield

Cadman, first performed at the Metropolitan Opera in March 1918 and brought back the following season. Articles and news flashes about the composer and his opera appeared in the press on an almost daily basis during the months prior to its two performances, June 24 and 28, 1926.

Shanewis was, we are told, the story of the love of an Indian maiden (the title role sung by an "authentic Indian Princess," Tsianina, also known as Redfeather) for a paleface (sung by the Met's Rafaelo Diaz, presumably authentic as well). The third lead, that of Shanewis' father, was taken by Os-ke-non-ton, "noted Mohawk Indian baritone." Gaetano Merola, artistic director of the San Francisco Opera, conducted, and the chorus was prepared by the same Alexander Bevani who had given us — as "impressario from the East" — the Bowl's very first opera, *Carmen*, in 1922.

The *Shanewis* reviews were unanimously enthusiastic, as was nearly every review of every ambitious artistic undertaking in the city at that time. Reviewing and civic boosterism were synonymous. Negative criticism in the press was regarded as rude, unseemly, above all discouraging to the fragile artistic sensibility of the city. Oh yes, and *Shanewis* "broke all attendance records" according to several sources. Failing to credit broken attendance records (rarely documented) was, likewise, considered rude.

The aforementioned Goossens opera evenings did indeed prove to be favorable harbingers. The 1930s was *the* decade of opera at the Bowl, which was most likely then the liveliest summer opera venue in the entire country.

Newspaper reviews remained at once simple-minded and highfalutin', to wit the following from the *Los Angeles Record* of August 28, 1932: "Frederick Stock drew his batonic curtain down on the Hollywood Bowl season when he conducted *Samson and Dalila*... It was a night never to be forgotten. First the large audience, knowing many months would pass before it would assemble again, gave the opera its undivided attention and enthusiastic support... Then the opera itself, with Paul Althouse as Samson and Clemence Gifford as Dalila. Both did fine work and the love duet was, of course, outstanding."

1933 was chockablock with arias, sung by Isobel Baillie, Richard Crooks, Grace Moore, Queena Mario, John Charles Thomas, Richard Bonelli, and others, but not even a potted opera. Then suddenly, in 1934, came concert versions of *Cavalleria rusticana*, *Pagliacci*, and *Carmen* on separate evenings. Nelson Eddy won an instant following as the dashing Escamillo of that *Carmen* under Pietro Cimini, who would become a fixture at the Bowl and in the Southland as conductor, accompanist, impresario, and vocal coach, retiring only a year before his death in 1971 at age 97.

Following Tibbett's example, Eddy returned in a matter of weeks to sing "Wotan's Farewell" under Sir Hamilton Harty. The operatic world was Eddy's for the taking, but his easygoing, all-American manner and good looks got in the way. Radio and film beckoned irresistibly, and instead of assuming the Wagnerian winged helmet and eyepatch, Eddy donned buckskins and powdered wigs (on separate occasions) for a string of hugely profitable period film musicals, usually co-starring the ravishing Jeanette MacDonald, who would, in her own later Bowl appearances, set a record unlikely ever to be surpassed: a total of seven arias from French opera, not one of them "Depuis le jour."

The 1934 concert *Carmen* had Marina Koshetz, Rachmaninoff's favorite interpreter of his songs, in the title role. Koshetz would also set up shop here as a teacher. The performance was sufficiently successful at the box office that the decision was made to *open* the following Bowl season with an opera: a non-stellar, as it turned out, concert *Aida*, led by Cimini. Hard on the heels of the '35 *Aida* came the Bowl's first full Wagner opera, a concert *Lohengrin*, conducted by Richard Lert, and two weeks later, *La traviata*, under Cimini, and then an English-language *Eugene Onegin* of Tchaikovsky. In each instance, the dailies' critics remained enthusiastic and for a time avoided the numbers game, preferring instead to inform that the events were "well attended" or that "the audience was large."

To many observers the big show of summer '36 was not a complete opera, but an opera singer: the fetching, wildly popular French coloratura Lily Pons with her future husband, conductor

Left: *Shanewis* composer
Charles Wakefield Cadman.

Right: Mezzo-soprano
Carmela Ponselle greets
conductor Pierre Monteux,
arriving by train for concerts
at the Hollywood Bowl.

André Kostelanetz, in tow for one of the Bowl's more believable attendance busters. Pons' arias included her signature "Bell Song" from *Lakmé*.

1936 brought another *Pagliacci* (one-acters were teamed with ballets or choral excerpts from operas for a full evening's entertainment) and '37 produced a *Carmen* featuring the Met's Bruna Castagna as the cigarette-smoking hussy, Cimini conducting, and another Bowl regular, the San Francisco Opera's Armando Agnini, as stage director. Castagna's other specialty, Azucena in *Il trovatore* (the first and only Bowl staging of Verdi's thriller), followed, and before the summer was out came another first for the Bowl, a staged *Madama Butterfly*, with Hizi Koyke, "the diminutive Japanese singing star," according to the program, as Cio-Cio-San.

Opera at the Bowl meant opera of the popular, hit-filled sort: *Carmen, Madama Butterfly, La bohème, La traviata,* and *Cavalleria rusticana* and *I Pagliacci* ultimately appearing with the greatest frequency. But financing was occasionally available for riskier business, as long as it provided the opportunity for visual spectacle and/or large forces, in keeping with Edwin Schallert's perceptive comments regarding that first *Carmen*. Thus, in 1937 we had Smetana's approachable but relatively esoteric *The Bartered Bride* (in English, as were most of the non-repertory operas), and Borodin's *Prince Igor* (in Russian) was staged in '39.

Sixteen Bowl seasons might have seemed merely a dress rehearsal for the opening fusillade of summer '38: a fully (and then some) staged *Walküre,* the operatic counterpart in its scenic lavishness and artistic reach to Max Reinhardt's celebrated 1934 Bowl production of Shakespeare's *A Midsummer Night's Dream.*

The *Walküre* cast was impressive indeed: Maria Jeritza as Brünnhilde, Paul Althouse as Siegmund, and Friedrich Schorr as Wotan. Richard Hageman, a seasoned Wagnerian but better known as the composer of such salon hit songs as "Do Not Go My Love" and "At the Well," was the conductor. The critics raved, so to speak, none more ecstatically than the nonsense- and *non sequitur-*prone Carl Bronson of the *Herald*: "One of the most remarkable audiences of distinction and musical quality that has ever at one time graced the mountainous tiers of seats and boxes... came early and loitered late. Distinguished citizens and celebrities from London, Paris, Berlin, and elsewhere abroad hobnobbed with equally distinguished notables from all over the United States and Los Angeles, and over all was the dominant tone of the new world and Old Glory waving in the breeze.

"The scene down front, across the sea of waving heads to the orchestral pit, was as unusual as the impressiveness of the occasion warranted. As suddenly as the switch of an impulse was the reaction of the thousands as the darkness which had until that vital instant beveiled the temporary forest of action merged into an eerie twilight when Richard Hageman lifted his deft baton high and led the Philharmonic Orchestra in the sweep of the instrumental storm..."

Bronson proceeded to praise the singers to the balmy skies but neglected to mention that live horses, allotted to apprentice, presumably non-singing, Valkyries careened down the hillsides for the "Ride" at the start of Act III. *Walküre* might have been the Bowl's shining operatic hour (or three or four).

Jeritza wasn't finished for the summer, returning for Santuzza in *Cavalleria rusticana*, which elicited the following from Bronson: "The Hollywood Bowl again bulged with a capacity audience...extending to the surrounding hilltops, applauding the performance... so unanimously as to testify to the fact that everybody both saw and heard... This improved adjustment to the acoustical properties of the wide-spreading amphitheater makes one section practically as choice as another..." And of Jeritza herself, "She was soft, she was loud, she was purring and suddenly catish [sic], and all that Mascagni dreamed into the role and much more was brought out as a film is gradually developed in the chemicals of art."

Next, perhaps anticlimactically in the eyes of posterity, came a well-attended, well-received, staged *Barbiere di Siviglia*, with John Charles Thomas as Figaro. Isabel Morse Jones' review in the *Times* gives one pause: she wrote that the performance was "without amplification and with its delicate pianissimi was a complete success... heard by 20,000 people."

Still in 1938: Puccini's *La bohème*, for the first time at the Bowl; and a reprise of Hizi Koyke's *Butterfly*, of which Jones noted, "the adjusting of the microphones annoyed some front-seat patrons."

Before the summer was out, there would be a second Wagnerian triumph, without benefit of horses or scenery, when Kirsten Flagstad joined the Philharmonic and its music director, Otto Klemperer, in arias from the master's operas for which (Bronson again) "The audience evidently exceeded in numbers and in enthusiasm any previous crowd ever to swarm the hillsides." Jones of the *Times* observed rather nicely that Flagstad was "no prima donna in the accepted sense... she stands unmoving before the audience with completely disarming and simple grace. She is the perfect instrument of song."

Jones was in loftiest Elizabethan fettle, however, in 1939 for Nicolai's little-known (outside the German-speaking world) *The Merry Wives of Windsor*. "Hollywood Bowl did play a play with wondrous music faire" and continued with a barrage of "methinks," "comely wenches," and the like, before getting to the most succulent morsel of the evening, her report that "scurvy knaves threw a cigarette into the canvas cover of a hot klieg light down in front and the resultant fire caused much smoke and excitement just as the lusty voiced choir of villagers, carefully drilled by Hugo Strelitzer, came on stage...." Humperdinck's *Hansel and Gretel* (not yet a "children's opera" in those days) dropped in that season and *Prince Igor* made his appearance — not on the same evening — before another celebrated vocalist, Lotte Lehmann, joined Klemperer and the Philharmonic for some Wagner and Richard Strauss. A strange operatic season at the Bowl, with three such offbeat works comprising the agenda.

The failure of *Merry Wives*, *H & G*, and *Igor* with audiences — the critics, however, still rarely had a discouraging word — added to the tepid reception accorded Flotow's *Martha* (at the end of the previous, otherwise exciting but very expensive, season) may have occasioned a rethinking of the Bowl's priorities. Thus, in 1940 we had only a *Carmen*, with the popular Gladys Swarthout in the title role — and, according to Bronson, "23,000 patrons, the greatest audience ever to hear a grand opera" — and big-name singers in concert, among them Pons, Thomas, and Flagstad. But '41 again began with an opera, *Madama Butterfly*, in which (according to Bronson) "the Philharmonic played...the queerly tinted, amorous music of the score divinely as Maestro Pietro Cimini waved his sensitively rhythmed arms...."

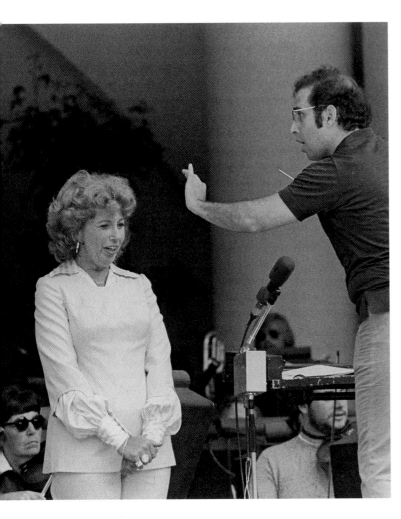

Further to that *Butterfly*, Mrs. Leiland Atherton Irish, doyenne of the Southern California Symphony Association, was part of the "throng in attendance" and remarked to the *Times*, "We needed only some white asbestos on top of one of those background mountains to make it look like Fujiyama and then our audience would surely have believed they were in Japan."

The 1941 *Traviata*, starring Jarmila Novotna, Jan Peerce, and Bonelli, had in the bit part of Dr. Grenvil a former Bowl usher named George Burnson — né Burnstein — who, with yet another name change, to George London, would later make his impressive operatic mark.

With the war on in Europe, even more American singers were given chances throughout the country and particularly at the Bowl. Among the most brilliant in '41 was Helen Traubel, who became the Bowl's reigning female Wagnerian — the incomparable Lauritz Melchior had already become the top male the preceding summer — when she sang Isolde's "Liebestod" and the Immolation Scene from *Götterdämmerung* under John Barbirolli.

During the first wartime summer, 1942, young Risë Stevens joined the Bowl's roster of eminent Carmens, but only in excerpts, and in '45 there was a staged *Cavalleria rusticana*, with Dusolina Giannini as Santuzza. Wartime seasons brought to the Bowl such luminaries as Marian Anderson and Ezio Pinza, and a towering "local boy from USC," Jerry (later Jerome) Hines.

1946, the first postwar summer and the Bowl's 25th anniversary season, was launched by a fancy production of *Carmen*, preceded by Gov. Earl Warren's exhortation to the audience to "turn from thoughts of carnage and destruction to those

Beverly Sills in rehearsal with conductor Lawrence Foster.

Kathleen Battle in concert, David Zinman on the podium.

elements of civilization which build and enrich life — elements which are fostered by the events held in this beautiful Hollywood Bowl." Marguerita Sylva, the 1922 Carmen, was a guest of honor.

The production, with Winifred Heidt as Carmen and Ramón Vinay her Don José, was conducted by Leopold Stokowski — the only opera he would ever grace at the Bowl, largely as a favor to his pal Boris Morros, the show's producer. Morros held various positions of power in the film industry and in 1946 was director of music for Paramount Pictures. Later, he would win another kind of renown as a snitch for the House Committee on Un-American Activities.

It would subsequently be revealed — most sensationally by Morros himself in his published autobiography, filmed in 1960 as *Man on a String*, starring Ernest Borgnine — that the gregarious, well-placed, Russian-born Morros, who was privy to all sorts of incriminating chat on both sides of the Iron Curtain, had been a spy in the employ of the FBI. Among those about whom he gathered information was the former actress and singer (Bowl '57, under Fritz Reiner) Helen Gahagan Douglas, who would in 1950 be vilified and then trounced by Richard M. Nixon in her bid to become California's junior senator.

1946 closed with *Pagliacci*, a vehicle for the venerated Giovanni Martinelli on the eve of his retirement from the stage. 1947 was distinguished by a fresh, non-singing voice at the Bowl: the *Times'* newly-acquired critic, transplanted Chicagoan Albert Goldberg (1898-1990), who brought literacy and a keen musical intelligence to Los Angeles journalism.

Goldberg's first summer also brought a daunting assignment, reviewing the debut of soprano Margaret Truman, daughter of the President of the United States. Harry Truman took a keen interest in his daughter's career and a few years later would write to Paul Hume of the *Washington Post*: "I have read your lousy review of Margaret's concert... Some day I hope to meet you. When that happens you'll need a new nose, a lot of beefsteak for black eyes, and perhaps a supporter below."

It was, even by Bowl standards, an event. As a *Times* cityside reporter observed, "Cars began arriving at 3 PM...although Margaret Truman's first public concert was almost six hours away. Finding the gates weren't open, the uninitiated sat in their cars or strolled up the steep pathway. Others, wiser, brought lunch and checkerboards. All day long sweet old ladies had swamped the Bowl Association's switchboards: 'Tell the dear girl I'm too ill to come but I wish her well.' The President's daughter arrived two full hours before concert time in a long black limousine. Following was a similar car filled with secret service men. She wore a long white coat and beneath a white turban on her ash blond hair peeked a prosaic curler."

Goldberg's dignified review noted that, "The longest mile in the world is the 50 feet from the stage door to center stage. It is a measurable distance for any experienced artist. For a debutante with the eyes of the nation focused upon her, it could very well be the road to Gethsemane. Yet, if there were any perturbations in the tall, slender, blond young woman in white who advanced to the cordial welcoming applause to take her place before the orchestra last night, it was not evident to the naked eye. She was the very image of poise and assurance and even the most skeptical critic had at once to award her a bright, golden 'A' for courage."

Goldberg went on to award her something like a C- for her singing of arias by Mozart and Grétry, basing his judgment largely on her lack of experience and for exhibiting more technique (although that was not adjudged to be perfect, either) than expressivity. "What she may accomplish in the way of a career is entirely up to the young artist herself and also what she chooses to make of a voice possessing promise but which still needs skill and care in its guidance." Owen Callin, the critic of the *Herald*, trashed Truman's singing and condemned her presumptuousness, but gave her credit for daring to appear before an estimated 15,000 customers.

A couple of nights later, the Bowl first heard, and cheered, a 26-year-old tenor named Mario Lanza, of whom Goldberg wrote: "His voice is full and free, and something of the charming ingenuousness of his manner carries over into his singing. He is young and it is the sort of youth all the world loves." The engaging Philadelphian's performances of arias by Donizetti, Ciléa, and Puccini led Goldberg to conclude that "[Lanza's] is the sort of tenor voice that nearly every stage in the world has been yearning for…" Lanza, like Nelson Eddy, instead pursued the substantial monetary rewards of film. But unlike Eddy, the fiery, hard-living tenor would burn out early and die tragically at age 38.

Making his first Bowl podium appearances on those two memorable occasions and virtually ignored amid the hoopla was another Philadelphian (by adoption), Eugene Ormandy, who would finally win favorable notice the following season, for *Madama Butterfly* — Eleanor Steber, Peerce, and Bonelli were the principals — and a Wagner concert with Traubel and Melchior.

1949 brought to the Bowl the golden tenor of Jussi Bjoerling, but only one opera, a staged *Traviata*, with Compton's (and the Met's) youthful Nadine Conner and the reportedly ageless (at 59) John Charles Thomas. A 1950 *Faust* (staged) was well-received by the critics for the conducting of Artur Rodzinski, a former music director of the Los Angeles Philharmonic, and a cast that included Richard Tucker, Conner, and Hines. But it didn't draw, not by pre-war standards, anyway, in the now 16,000-seat amphitheater. In all fairness, not much of anything seemed to pull them in that summer, unhappily also a time when expenses were soaring.

Trouble was brewing, and it exploded at the very start of the '51 season, in the outwardly innocuous form of *Die Fledermaus*. The Johann Strauss bon-bon would surely bring about a reversal in the Bowl's sagging fortunes; it had everything going for it, in the minds of its producers: favorable advance publicity provided by its recent monster success (although with a different, far more starry cast) at the staid Metropolitan Opera, using the same English-language version by Ruth and Thomas Martin; staging (here) entrusted to a pair of respected pros, ex-opera tenor Vladimir Rosing and film comic Sig Arno; and a cast that included movie vamp Yvonne De Carlo complementing such veteran opera performers as Marina Koshetz and John Brownlee. Even the conductor had, someone assumed, mass appeal: Franz Waxman, fresh from an Academy Award for his score for the Gloria Swanson-Billy Wilder *Sunset Boulevard*.

Alas, during its five-performance run (even in its operatic heyday, the Bowl had never ventured more than two performances of any work), audiences seemed not so much to leave humming the elaborate sets as snarling them.

Goldberg commented on the production's lack of wit, its visual ponderousness, and variable vocal quality. The *Herald's* Callin remarked on the sparse audience and its timid applause, while his paper's nonjudgmental society editor presented a lengthy list of the toffs who attended, preceded by the democratic notice that "social and film leaders and music loving Jane and John Does listened attentively."

At the end of the *Fledermaus* run, the Southern California Symphony Association announced that it was aborting the season. The Bowl was broke, a consequence of problems born well before this fabulously flopping *Fledermaus*. Dorothy Buffum Chandler spearheaded the ensuing rescue effort.

Starting in '52, the Hollywood Bowl was a leaner operation. Part of the cost-cutting involved the quasi-elimination (again) of traditionally money-sucking opera. Staged operas were out, and concert presentations were drastically reduced in number. The Bowl story ever since — a few flareups excepted — is the story of singers rather than productions, just as it had been in the '20s.

Among the voices added to the roster since the early-'50s have been Leonard Warren, Bidu Sayão, Robert Merrill, Patrice Munsel, Giorgio Tozzi, Elisabeth Schwarzkopf, Hilde Gueden, Roberta Peters, Birgit Nilsson (who made her American debut with a Wagner program at the Bowl on August 9, 1956), Anna Moffo, Renata Tebaldi, Joan Sutherland, Leontyne Price, Mary Costa, Marni Nixon, Eileen Farrell, Marilyn Horne, George Shirley, Jess Thomas, Norman Treigle, Beverly Sills, Teresa Stratas, Jessye Norman, Sherrill Milnes, Montserrat Caballé, Kathleen Battle, Christa Ludwig, Shirley Verrett , Frederica Von Stade, Florence Quivar, Dmitri Hvorostovsky, and June Anderson — and each of The Three Tenors (José Carreras, Plácido Domingo, Luciano Pavarotti), relatively early in their careers and as clearly distinguishable, individual entities. Many of those on this by-no-means-complete list appeared under the baton of Zubin Mehta, who, however, has never led a full opera at the Bowl.

Concert opera returned briefly in 1953 with, wouldn't you know?, *Carmen.* The poor attendance inspired operatically-bereft '54 and '55 summers. Both, however, brought us Dorothy Kirsten singing "Depuis le jour," under distinguished if unlikely conductors, Adrian Boult and Georg Solti. There was sterner stuff from the underrated Inge Borkh (the *Salome* finale and "In questa reggia" from *Turandot),* Wagner from Marjorie Lawrence, and from the sublime to the sublimely ridiculous, evenings with the Alberghetti Performing Circus — telegenic teenaged coloratura Anna Maria and her musical siblings and parents. The '55 season ended with dignity, the young Leontyne Price singing Verdi and joined by William Warfield, her husband then, in *Porgy and Bess* highlights.

1956 was a year of some vocal giants: Marian Anderson, returning after more than a decade's absence, Nilsson, Tebaldi, Price again. But the only full-length opera presentations between '57 and '62 were single performances of *Carmen* (in 1959), *Butterfly* (1960), and *Bohème* (1961), none particularly well-received by either audiences or critics. Full-length opera could no longer pay its way at the Bowl. But *singing* could be profitable, even with a pricey attraction such as Joan Sutherland or Beverly Sills, the latter in fact first heard at the Bowl in 1962, a few years before her career took off.

Whether opera did pay its way in 1971 is doubtful, but for some quirkily wonderful reason, it was there to a degree no longer deemed possible. First was a *Traviata* with three glittering principals, Beverly Sills, the up-and-coming Plácido Domingo, and the *nonpareil* Verdi baritone, Sherrill Milnes. The conductor was James Levine, on his way to becoming a dominant force on the international operatic scene. Next came an evening devoted to substantial excerpts from Richard Strauss' *Der Rosenkavalier,* with Erich Leinsdorf at the helm and Tatiana Troyanos' Octavian. Finally, a big gamble that paid off (artistically, at any rate): the return of the dread *Fledermaus,* this time in concert form.

Martin Bernheimer, by then the *Times'* chief music critic, praised the performance for displaying "genuine and infectious high spirits," commented on "the tightness, brightness and sparkle" of

Leinsdorf's conducting and the "fervor and finesse" of George Shirley's Alfred, and admired Clarice Carson, who brought to Rosalinde's music a "luscious, full-throated dramatic soprano."

1972 started festively with a concert *Aida*, conducted by Levine, which provided the occasion for Jessye Norman's much-anticipated American operatic debut. Bernheimer's review of Norman was cautiously favorable, noting her "gorgeous lyric spinto, obvious affinity for the arching Verdian line" and "rather uneven technique." He was unabashed, however, in his admiration for Mignon Dunn, "an Amneris of grandiose passion and vocal opulence," and for the "precision, flexibility and freshness" of Roger Wagner's Los Angeles Master Chorale. Attendance was officially tabulated at 12,000-plus in a house that now seated 18,000.

Within a month the Bowl, on an operatic roll, presented Verdi's *Rigoletto*, with Louis Quilico in the title role, Carol Neblett's Gilda, and, as the Duke, a young Spaniard, José Carreras, whom Albert Goldberg described as "a lyric tenor who is slender and handsome, with a voice of suavity and reasonable power that can whip up ardor and emotion in 'Parmi veder le lagrime,' careless nonchalance in 'Questa o quella,' top off a graceful 'La donna è mobile' with a ringing high B, and decisively dominate the quartet. That kind of singing is apt to be around often in the future." Had the audience known beforehand, more than the 6,000-odd might have attended.

Two ambitious projects were ventured in 1973. Mozart's *Don Giovanni* was performed in an uncut, semi-staged version. Levine conducted a cast that included Thomas Stewart's Don and Jessye Norman as Elvira, the Leporello of Ezio Flagello, and a future Don of distinction, James Morris, as the Commendatore. Interestingly, it drew twice the audience of the '72 *Rigoletto* — and the approval of the *Times'* Daniel Cariaga.

But the event of the summer took place on August 25, a *Bohème*, semi-staged again and this time conducted by Lawrence Foster. Bernheimer wrote, with wry affection: "*La bohème* is customarily dominated by the diva who gets to cough and simper and tear our hearts out as the consumptive little artificial flower maker, Mimi. Saturday night at Hollywood Bowl, however, the opera belonged to her poet-tenor boyfriend [Rodolfo]... Luciano Pavarotti. He is a singer with extraordinarily good instincts, and the vocal endowments to make them count. He clearly knows what he is doing, and he does it with tremendous charm as well as overwhelming authority... he produced an endless stream of sweet, poised, lustrous tone... phrased with a freshness that illuminated even the most familiar passages, and he kept that incredible voice warm and vibrant and free..." Mimi, the heavily-promoted Katia Ricciarelli, didn't come in for such kind treatment.

In 1975 another splendidly-equipped tenor, Jon Vickers, offered arias by Verdi, Wagner, Bizet, and Leoncavallo, replacing a cancelled performance by Pavarotti. Vickers was present again in '81 for a full-evening's Wagner but not of the familiar sort: a concert presentation of Act II of the relatively recondite *Parsifal*, conducted by Leinsdorf and with Troyanos as Kundry.

As part of the Bowl's gutsy Stravinsky Centenary Festival presented in 1982, a semi-staged, thrillingly sung *Oedipus Rex*, with a very young and gifted Jerry Hadley in the title role, Florence Quivar's haunted Jocasta, and the heroic Creon of Lenus Carlson is remembered with particular fondness. Michael Tilson Thomas conducted the Philharmonic and the men of the Los Angeles Master Chorale, both at peak form. The audience, unfortunately, was minuscule.

More up the audience's alley, Pavarotti has returned many times, to ever larger houses, including 1984, the year of the L.A. Olympics, which also featured the re-appearance of another celebrated no-show, Spanish soprano Montserrat Caballé, who had made her several-times-delayed Bowl bow in 1978, sharing the stage then with Marilyn Horne for a rousing "Prima Donna Gala."

1985 was notable for Kiri Te Kanawa's house debut, singing Mozart and various Strausses, and for a concert *Bohème* presented by the orchestra of the lamented Los Angeles Philharmonic Institute, conducted by Tilson Thomas, with a cast, as attractive visually as it was vocally, headed by Roberta Alexander, Richard Leech, and Dale Duesing.

The Institute in fact gave us the last full opera to be heard in the Bowl for nearly a decade when Sir Charles Groves conducted *Fidelio* in 1986. Like its successor in 1995, Mozart's *The Magic Flute* from Peter Maag and members of his Bottega in Treviso, that *Fidelio* stressed youth and promise rather than audience-grabbing names.

In recent years, John Mauceri (with extensive opera background, including Scottish Opera and Teatro Regio in Turin) has augmented the concert schedule with programs of operatic fare. These have included young singers in extended scenes (rather than isolated arias) from popular operas — for example, Jane Eaglen as Brünnhilde in Act II of *Die Walküre* in 1994 (with Robert Hale her Wotan) and Priscilla Baskerville and Florence Quivar in Act II of *Aida* in 1995 — a return to the programs presented by Eugene Goossens in the late-'20s, the dawning of the Bowl's operatic heyday.

Oedipus Rex starring Florence Quivar and Jerry Hadley, conducted by Michael Tilson Thomas, 1982.

HOLLYWOOD AND THE BOWL

BY LISA MITCHELL

The concert has just started, as a handsome movie star who "seems to have had that one extra cocktail" refuses to let a photographer take his picture. After all, he explains, "This is the *Hollywood Bowl*!" Following a skirmish when a flashbulb pops anyway, the actor settles into his box seat. But... someone else isn't respecting the sanctity of the place: a wide-eyed young woman several rows behind him is talking. Turning to look over his right shoulder, he makes eye contact with her and gives her a brief "Shhhh!" sign.

He is Norman Maine, washing a glamorous film career down the drain with alcohol; *she* is Esther Blodgett, lately come west to be that "one in a hundred thousand" who will make it in the movies. The picture is, of course, David O. Selznick's *A Star Is Born* (1937), directed by William Wellman, blessed by the presence of the brilliant Fredric March as Maine and Janet Gaynor as Blodgett (later Vicky Lester).

The story of an ascending actress and her descending mentor has been told, with variations, before — in 1932's *What Price Hollywood?*, also produced by Selznick, directed by George Cukor — and after, in 1954's remake of *A Star Is Born*, with Cukor again at the helm. (Though a Frank Pierson-directed picture used the same title in 1976, the milieu was rock music.)

But it is the 1937 film, dreamy in its early Technicolor, that most affectingly presents Hollywood as both magical and significant. Nowhere is this more apparent than in the scene at the Bowl. "Look at all the people!" Esther says. "Everybody in the world." Seeing the shimmering navy blue night, the golden glow of the shell, the expanse of the outdoor audience, we feel her intoxication.

As one of three remaining landmarks — the others being the Chinese Theater and the Hollywood Sign — the Bowl has been used by movie companies to establish a Hollywood setting for seven decades. Only the Bowl, however, confers an element of refinement on a town sometimes derided as a cultural wasteland. And the Bowl alone has been able to be cinematically transported, as in *Saleslady* (1938), when it is seen as the site for a concert in Chicago.

Gene Kelly, José Iturbi, and Frank Sinatra share a piano in this scene from *Anchors Aweigh*, 1945.

A Midsummer Night's Dream,
directed by Max Reinhardt, 1934.

Set of *Robin Hood*, 1927, a production underwritten by William Farnum, Douglas Fairbanks, and Mary Pickford.

Shovel used (and signed) by Mary Pickford for the 1927 Easter-lily planting ceremony.

By and large, the Bowl has been in character, usually identified either by name or from a sign at its entrance, in numerous Hollywood films and in television shows from *The Beverly Hillbillies* to *Melrose Place*. Void of its usual crowds at night, it has played romantic background in such boy-seeks-girl vehicles as *Xanadu* (1980) and *Some Kind Of Wonderful* (1987).

A vacant-seated Bowl in broad daylight energizes the pre-title sequence of *Beaches* (1988), with spectacular footage of Frank Gehry's white fiberglass spheres in the shell for the opening shot. The film also offers glimpses of sidelines, as rehearsing pop star C.C. Bloom (Bette Midler) rushes off the stage into a waiting limo. For an earlier record showing more of the environs, there is *Jive Junction* (1943), in which high school musicians borrow instruments from the Bowl orchestra to win a band contest.

An empty Bowl in the afternoon has also served the weird (a lawyer reads a deceased magician's will to three survivors on a bare stage) in *Two On A Guillotine* (1965), and the winsome, as in two musical love stories, *Hollywood Hotel* (1938) and *Anchors Aweigh* (1945).

"You mean to say a person singing on that stage way down there can be heard all the way up here?" new-to-Hollywood Dick Powell (at the top of the hill) asks Rosemary Lane in *Hotel*. "I can prove it to you," she answers and runs down onto the stage to sing to him. (As it happens, the owner of the real Hollywood Hotel, Myra Hershey, was one of the owners of the property that became the site of the Hollywood Bowl.)

The Bowl scene in *Anchors Aweigh* is remarkable beyond the fun of watching sailors Gene Kelly and Frank Sinatra slide down the hill, then run down, down, down the aisles between groups of seats in perfect Technicolor sunshine. They have come to see José Iturbi, who is at the piano rehearsing for a concert, surrounded by dozens of young students accompanying him on their own pianos in forceful unison. Iturbi had been appearing at the Bowl for years, as both soloist and conductor.

Directed by George Sidney, the musical number is masterfully designed, with the camera slowing pulling back from the stage to encompass the entire shell, luxuriously panning along each young pianist, or shooting unusual angles of Iturbi's hands on the keyboard. Reverse shots play up the vastness of the ocean of seats as the boys scamper towards the camera, their movements accented perfectly by Iturbi's music.

To get the right sound for the great throng of pianos, Sidney — who plays four instruments himself and is a member of ASCAP — used just four pianists, among them Jakob Gimpel and André Previn, then multiplied their tracks. George Sidney's seeming fascination with the Bowl also may have found its way into the final scene of his *Holiday In Mexico* (1946), where Jane Powell sings "Ave Maria" at an open-air concert in a fantastical combination of the Hollywood Bowl and a Hispanic religious grotto.

The Bowl has shown up in musicals such as *It's A Great Feeling* (1949), mostly to supply Doris Day, Dennis Morgan, and Jack Carson with an interesting Hollywood locale. Though their hilltop perch is obviously on a Warner Bros. set — with an insert of the audience and shell in reverse angles

Scene from *The Symphony*, 1928.

Scene from *A Star is Born*, 1937.

— there is charming coverage of the real Bowl's entrance sign and trademark Muses sculpture as cars of the era drive in. There are also sweet moments showing the old ticket stand and the grounds as people climb the pathways to their seats.

The Bowl plays a meatier role in the light mystery, *Moonlight Murder* (1936), where an opera singer (Leo Carillo) is attacked by an insane composer (J. Carroll Naish) while rehearsing *Il trovatore*. It has welcomed the adventuresome Katharine Hepburn who, having refused a stunt double, landed a hot-air balloon herself in front of the stage during a performance of the *1812 Overture* in *Olly Olly Oxen Free* (1978). And while its streets are not mean, it is no stranger to such film noir classics as *Double Indemnity* (1944).

"One night we went up into the hills behind the Hollywood Bowl," insurance salesman Walter Neff (Fred MacMurray) says in voice-over. We see him wearing a hat as he sits on the ground leaning against a tree, having a smoke. The lit-up shell in the distance below is small, the only bright spot in the dark night around Neff and Lola Dietrichson (Jean Heather). In the film, Lola is the daughter of the man Phyllis Dietrichson (Barbara Stanwyck) was married to until Neff helped Phyllis bump him off.

Of all Bowl movies, *The Symphony* (1928 — also known as *Jazz Mad*) is of particular historical value. It is the story of an old-world composer in America who is despondent because his classical work is unwanted in the jazz age. He is played by the venerable character actor Jean Hersholt — famous for his role as "Dr. Christian," and highly respected off-screen for his many humanitarian activities. Hersholt would become one of the directors of the Hollywood Bowl Association and its president (1950-51) during a summer of crisis.

In *The Symphony*, the melancholy composer is taken to a concert at the Bowl (filmed during a live performance although the Bowl is never named, as the action takes place in New York), and is revived by hearing his long-lost masterpiece on the program. The music is shown being played by the real Hollywood Bowl Symphony Orchestra, led by the real Bowl conductor, Alfred Hertz. When the composer walks onto the stage, Hertz — who has been described as a combination of Daddy Warbucks and one of the Smith Brothers of coughdrop fame — steps down, relinquishing his baton to Hersholt, who actually conducts.

Unfortunately, we can only imagine how the music sounded under Hersholt's hand, or Hertz', because the film was completely silent! This is especially strange since many pictures released at that time had synchronized sound, and that sound was almost always used for musical passages. As *Variety* emphasized, if ever a scenario cried for synchronization, it was *The Symphony*.

A reviewer for *The Hollywood Film Spectator* waxed rhapsodic over Hertz being in the cast. "I have listened to his music that swelled beyond me to the hills that sleep beyond the Bowl," he wrote. "But not even the moon that looked down upon me, nor the stars that bejewelled the moon's domain, bewitched me into imagining him to be a movie actor... Also it was a clever idea to use the Bowl itself. It is not often that we see thirty thousand unpaid extras in one picture."

Another Bowl conductor, the much-lionized Leopold Stokowski, appears in person in such non-Bowl films as *The Big Broadcast of 1937* (1936) and *One Hundred Men And A Girl* (1937), he is represented by parody in *Music For Madame* (1937), which does contain scenes at the Bowl. Reviews praised the caricature by Alan Mowbray as "the famous conductor, Leon Rodowsky" in a plot that involved moviemaking, jewel thievery, and the successful debut of tenor Nino Martini at the Hollywood Bowl.

Filming *Anchors Aweigh*, 1945.

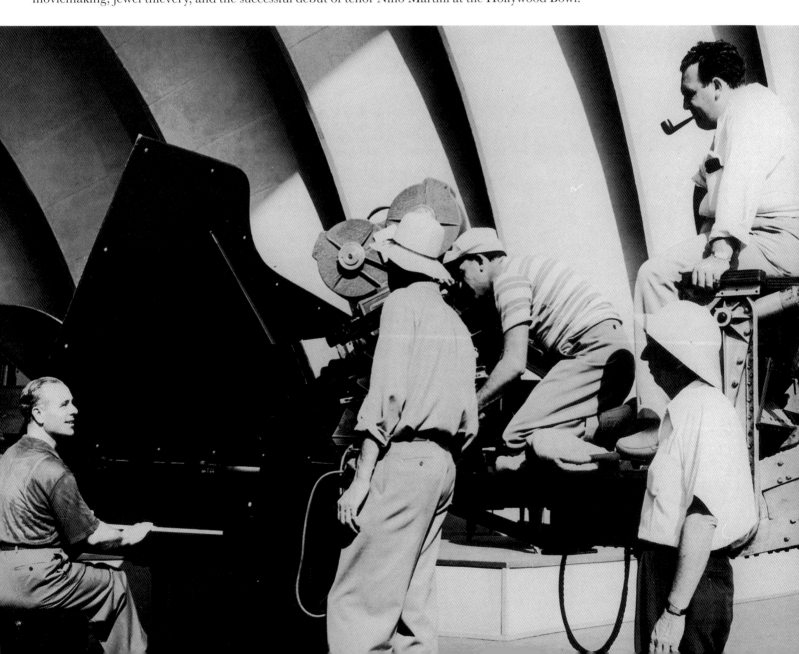

The Los Angeles Philharmonic and Warner Bros. present

BUGS BUNNY on Broadway

at the Hollywood Bowl

Starring
BUGS BUNNY
and
GEORGE
DAUGHERTY
conducting the
LOS ANGELES
PHILHARMONIC

also starring
ELMER FUDD
DAFFY DUCK
PORKY PIG
GIOVANNI JONES
and GRANNY

featuring a
birthday tribute to
Chuck Jones

Friday,
September 18, 1992
8:00 p.m.

George Daugherty rehearses with the Los Angeles Philharmonic for "Bugs Bunny on Broadway At The Hollywood Bowl."

Stokowski's persona is also invoked in Chuck Jones' classic cartoon, *Long-Haired Hare* (1949), in which Bugs Bunny sabotages tenor "Giovanni Jones" during a concert at the Bowl. It all started when the singer's practice session was disrupted by a certain rabbit warbling "What'll They Do on a Rainy Night in Rio?" while plucking a banjo. When Giovanni breaks the banjo, Bugs gets a harp. When that too is destroyed, and then a tuba, Bugs declares, "This means *war*!"

After making the Bowl's shell reverberate by hitting it with a mallet, and having the tenor sign an autograph with a stick of sizzling dynamite, Bugs suddenly appears in formal attire, wearing a white wig. "Leopold!" everyone in the orchestra proclaims. "Leopold!" echoes the evening's awe-struck conductor, who abdicates his podium to the renowned maestro. Bugs, now conducting with elaborate hand movements, makes Giovanni hold a note so long that the shell cracks and comes crashing down on him.

In a splendid case of life imitating [animation] art, Bugs returned to the field of his triumph in September 1992 and July 1994 via "Bugs Bunny On Broadway At The Hollywood Bowl." The musically-themed antics of Bugs and his cartoon confreres, projected on an enormous screen, were supported by the Los Angeles Philharmonic playing the scores live, under conductor George Daugherty. Both programs offered *Long-Haired Hare* as well as that other tip of Jones' hat to the Bowl, *Rabbit of Seville* (1950).

Author Joe Adamson, who has interviewed Jones extensively, notes that even the non-musical *Rabbit Punch* (1948) places its boxing match in a big open-air arena in the hills. Jones' predilection for the Bowl — indeed, his passion for classical music — has intertwining roots. "We used to live on

82

The Hollywood Bowl

Highland Avenue when I was a kid," Jones told Adamson, "and we could climb down the side of the hill and watch the whole Hollywood Bowl free. There was only one guard and he had a dog and the guard would always let us know when he was coming... We'd fade back into the bushes till he'd passed, and then go back and listen again."

Similarly, Joseph Barbera, creator with William Hanna of such Academy Award-winning musical cartoons as *The Cat Concerto* (1946) and *Johann Mouse* (1952), paid homage to "what's right in our back yard." Barbera had been president of the Greek Theatre, "but," he says, "when it came to doing a great music job, I moved [the location] to the Bowl." The result is the clever and tender gem, *Tom And Jerry At The Hollywood Bowl* (1950).

After a dazzling shot of a velvet blue night and a big golden shell, Tom — as the dignified conductor — proudly walks to the podium. The camera then pans over and down to a mouse hole which is an exact replica of the lit-up shell. Out rushes Jerry, hurriedly dressing (in a miniature copy of Tom's outfit), then scurrying up and onto Tom's music stand, where he blissfully joins him conducting the all-cat orchestra in the overture to... *Die Fledermaus*.

Tom tries to get rid of him, but as the waltz passage begins, he suddenly gets all mushy and starts dancing with Jerry. But after whirling off into a tuba, a hurting Tom is after Jerry again, adding insult to injury by using the mouse's little baton as a toothpick! In revenge, Jerry puts casters on the podium and sends Tom flying all the way down to Highland Avenue, where the Bowl sculpture is clearly visible. Because Jerry has disposed of all the musicians, Tom returns to pinch-hit for the entire orchestra (in one of the funniest bits of animation in the business), till he finishes in an exhausted heap.

It is in another comedy, the charming *Champagne for Caesar* (1950), that the Bowl does one of its most entertaining star turns. Near the end of the movie, after bookish Beauregard Bottomley (Ronald Colman) has given so many correct answers on the quiz show "Masquerade for Money," the neurotic sponsor, Burnbridge Waters (deliciously interpreted by Vincent Price) is ready to throw in the towel.

Convinced that Bottomley will soon take over his beloved Milady Soap ("The Soap That

HOLLYWOOD, CALIF.

Sanctifies") Company, Waters opts to go down in a blaze of glory by making the final radio/television broadcast the biggest show of all. "Book the Hollywood Bowl!" he cries. "Thousands and thousands of people! Fanfare and pageantry! The Twilight of the Gods!"

From that point on, other characters refer to the show itself as "The Bowl." The black and white footage of the gala is exhilarating. We see hundreds of people jamming the entrance and climbing the pathways. The shell is draped with a huge banner for "Milady Soap" and the dark night air is alive with shiny bubbles. The show's host, Happy Hogan (Art Linkletter), Waters, and Bottomley walk onto the stage and out towards the audience to a special platform. There, for "$40 million or nothing," Beauregard Bottomley can't remember his Social Security number.

The titular character of *Champagne for Caesar* — a dipsomaniacal parrot — was not present at that apocalyptic show. The emperor's name that he bore, however, has its own relationship to the saga of Hollywood and the Bowl.

In 1916, the tercentenary of Shakespeare's death, an outdoor production of *Julius Caesar* was given in Beachwood Canyon, just east of the Cahuenga Pass. The performance, benefitting the Actors Fund Of America, drew 40,000 people. The cast included such leading film players as William Farnum, Tully Marshall, Douglas Fairbanks, and Mae Murray, with Theodore Roberts (who would play Moses in Cecil B. De Mille's 1923 epic *The Ten Commandments*) as Caesar.

Properties were donated by such film industry pioneers as D.W. Griffith, Thomas Ince, Jesse Lasky, Mack Sennett, and Universal Film Corporation. Studio technicians built a facsimile of Rome on its Seven (Hollywood) Hills, which, in an extravagant lighting display, was lit in changing colors (white for day, blues and greens for night, reds for dawn and dusk) to dramatize the hillside actions of thousands of extras.

The presentation was "so stupendously successful," *Los Angeles Times* columnist Bill Henry wrote in a looking-back piece in July 1958, "that from it sprang the determination that Hollywood should have...a permanent outdoor amphitheatre such as blossomed into the Hollywood Bowl."

With the Hollywood film community's link to the Bowl having been forged even before there was a Bowl, the connections continued in various ways throughout their mutual — and individual — developments. A Thanksgiving pageant in November 1920, which has been called the "First production in the Hollywood Bowl," was directed by Lionel Barrymore. Lloyd Wright, the eldest son of Frank Lloyd Wright, designed shells and sets for the Bowl in the '20s. In creating his first music shell, Wright is said to have used lumber from the set he had built for Reginald De Koven's light opera, *Robin Hood*, a Bowl production for which the guarantors were William Farnum, Douglas Fairbanks, and Mary Pickford.

The *crème de la crème* of movie society held boxes at the Bowl, and, as it would be across the decades, the Bowl was *the* place to be seen — and photographed. Looking through programs from 1928, between advertisements for music instruction, The Pig 'n' Whistle Restaurants, Mt. Lowe, and The Roosevelt Hotel ("The Moving Picture Hotel"), we find listed among the boxholders for that season: C. Chaplin (#117), Mr. and Mrs. Cecil B. De Mille (#641), William De Mille (#736), Sid Grauman (#136), Alexander Korda (#113), Robert Z. Leonard (#143), Adolphe Menjou (#528), Conrad Nagel (#734), and Fay Wray (#861).

A full page in the third week of the 1928 program book displays a "Dedicatory Address for the Seventh Season of 'Symphonies Under the Stars' " by Conrad Nagel. The actor, who was a co-founder of the Academy of Motion Picture Arts and Sciences, welcomed Bowl attendees in an article acknowledging gratitude "to the Creator for His gifts to our little corner of His great universe."

In September 1934, 18 years after the Beachwood Canyon presentation of *Julius Caesar*, film stars were brushing up their Shakespeare in Max Reinhardt's sumptuous production of *A Midsummer*

Top left: Maurice Jarre
conducting his score for
Lawrence of Arabia.
Top right: David Raskin,
composer of "Laura."

Danny Kaye backstage with
Jean-Pierre Rampal and
Zubin Mehta.

Scene from *Some Kind of Wonderful*, 1987.

John Williams is accompanied by an old friend.

Filmed at the Hollywood Bowl

THE SYMPHONY (1928); also released as JAZZ MAD
MOONLIGHT MURDER (1936)
A STAR IS BORN (1937) *
MUSIC FOR MADAME (1937)
HOLLYWOOD HOTEL (1938) *
SALESLADY (1938)
JIVE JUNCTION (1943) *
DOUBLE INDEMNITY (1944) *
ANCHORS AWEIGH (1945) *
IT'S A GREAT FEELING (1949) *
LONG-HAIRED HARE (1949) *
RABBIT OF SEVILLE (1950) *
TOM AND JERRY AT
THE HOLLYWOOD BOWL (1950) *
CHAMPAGNE FOR CAESAR (1950) *
TWO ON A GUILLOTINE (1965)
OLLY OLLY OXEN FREE (1978); also released as
THE GREAT BALLOON ADVENTURE
THE MAN WITH BOGART'S FACE (1980)
XANADU (1980) *
SOME KIND OF WONDERFUL (1987) *
BEACHES (1988) *
JIMMY HOLLYWOOD (1994) *
* available on video

Night's Dream. In the cast were John Lodge — at the height of his screen career, having just appeared opposite Marlene Dietrich in *The Scarlet Empress* (1934), William Farnum, Leif Erickson, Walter Connolly, Sterling Holloway, Olivia de Havilland, Evelyn Venable, and Mickey Rooney. Fred Niblo, who had directed such dynamic action pictures as *Ben-Hur* (1926), was casting director; Theodore Kosloff — dancer/actor/choreographer in and for dozens of films, most notably Cecil B. De Mille's — was ballet master.

Reinhardt had been one of Germany's most important theatrical producer-directors and had greatly influenced German and international cinema. "He worked out a torch parade for [the play's] last act," his son Gottfried Reinhardt later wrote, "stepping to Mendelssohn's Wedding March, from the heights of the Hollywood hills to the bottom of the valley.... It did not concern him that in southern California's tinder-dry vegetation, that constituted a fire hazard of the first order."

The premiere on September 17 coincided with the opening night of the Trocadero on the Sunset Strip, where many playgoers flocked after the performance. *Dream* was a box-office hit and Reinhardt went on to produce and co-direct (with William Dieterle) his film version of it in 1935 — with Olivia de Havilland and Mickey Rooney reprising their roles of Hermia and Puck for the cameras.

Hollywood's involvement with the Bowl went beyond stage dramas and movie locations. Dennis Morgan, Alexis Smith (who had danced at the Bowl with the Adolph Bolm Ballet as a young girl) and others in the film business participated in Easter sunrise services... a Bowl souvenir booklet from 1960 includes a stunning photograph from an earlier undated period of Mary Pickford in ethereal dress and pose (an angel? the Madonna?), complete with halo. And on July 1, 1946, the Bowl was even the arena for a Conference of Studio Unions in which a capacity crowd of members from eleven locals met to discuss a strike against producers.

World War II engendered a number of benefits, though even before America entered the war, Robert Vogel, head of MGM's International Department, arranged a concert for the Finnish and Polish War Relief Fund at the Bowl on May 1, 1940. "Symphony Versus Swing" offered Stokowski and the Philharmonic on the first half of the bill, with Benny Goodman and his band on the second.

There were War Bond variety shows and star-studded "Music For The Wounded" concerts — one evening boasted Stokowski, Igor Stravinsky, and Sigmund Romberg, all as conductors. At a "Star Show For The U.S.O.," the audience of 30,000 contributors and servicemen (who were welcomed by Norma Shearer) saw such screen personalities as Cary Grant, Irene Dunne, Barbara Stanwyck, Tyrone Power, Bette Davis, Stan Laurel and Oliver Hardy, and Orson Welles. John and Lionel Barrymore did a skit with Rudy Vallee, and Hattie McDaniel sang "My Old Kentucky Home."

Of all fundraising interactions between the industry and the Bowl, perhaps none was more appropriate than a "Paramount Night of Stars." It was presented by Boris Morros, head of the studio's music department, on August 17, 1936, and featured Stokowski (in his Bowl debut, and at the time appearing in two Paramount pictures), Victor Young as an associate conductor, and the singing and dancing stars of *The Champagne Waltz* (1937).

Proceeds from the concert were, in the words of Paramount chairman Adolph Zukor, "to fill the continuous fund of the splendid Philharmonic Orchestra of Los Angeles... More than that, however, we wish to celebrate the fusion of the best in music with the best in motion pictures."

The fusion was far-reaching, as it has been going on for almost 75 years. In 1990 and 1991, Gary Essert of the American Cinematheque brought big-screen movies to the Hollywood Bowl, with one of the largest movie screens ever, augmenting presentation (of *Singin' in the Rain* and *The King and I*) with live dancers, cartoons, trailers, and other trappings of a traditional movieland event. Beginning in 1993, audiences have enjoyed watching movies shown on the Bowl's giant screen with live musical accompaniment, or a compendium of classic film scenes, as in 1995's commemorative concert, the "Centennial Celebration of the Moving Picture" with John Mauceri leading the Hollywood Bowl Orchestra.

In association with producer John Goberman, the Orchestra has accompanied projected scenes from such classics as *The Adventures of Robin Hood*, *Citizen Kane*, *North by Northwest*, *Oklahoma!*, *Things to Come*, and *The Wizard of Oz*, often with specially prepared reconstructions of the long-lost original music. Mauceri has given first public presentations of Max Steiner's overtures written for the world premieres of *King Kong* (1933) and *The Adventures of Mark Twain* (1944), and Erich Wolfgang Korngold's overture to *Juarez* (1939). He also helped restore parts of Miklós Rózsa's Academy Award-winning score to *Ben-Hur* (1959) and gave the first public performance of its overture in 35 years.

Over the decades, there have been concerts spotlighting different studios and their vocal artists, actors narrating in conjunction with choral and orchestral works, and continuing evenings of "Music of the Cinema." During its Silver Jubilee Season, the Bowl held its second "Motion Picture Academy Night," put on by the Academy's Music Branch on August 17, 1946. John Green conducted the Bowl Symphony Orchestra in a "Hit Parade of Academy Award-Winning Songs."

The most visible and enduring tie that binds the Bowl with the Academy — and, by extension, with Hollywood — is the "Oscar" statuette. The figure was crafted by George Maitland Stanley (1903-1970), the man who designed and sculpted the art deco fountain, 'The Muses', at the entrance to the Bowl. Cedric Gibbons, who made some original Oscar designs, had seen Stanley's work and hired the young sculptor to bring his sketches into form.

Stanley's largest Muse at the sculpture's prow, that masthead of the Bowl — strong, sturdy, but also elegant — is a more precious symbol of and for Hollywood now than at any time in its history. With so much having changed in the town, it is, rather like the Statue of Liberty, a reassuring keeper of the flame. As, of course, is the Bowl itself.

To quote Jimmy Alto (Joe Pesci) when he walks into a deserted Bowl one night in the Barry Levinson film *Jimmy Hollywood* (1994): "You can find better than this?" Alto, a would-be actor-cum-vigilante about to give himself up, needs "an appropriate setting" in which he can have himself videotaped making a grand farewell speech. "Someplace," he says, "that speaks 'Hollywood'... The Hollywood Bowl! That's it!"

Perhaps it is the story of Julio Gonzalez that says it all best. When Gonzalez, now an archivist for the Music Center Operating Company in Los Angeles, was a young man in his native Cuba, it was the Bowl that meant "Hollywood" to him more than any other landmark. And how did he know of it? Through books? Magazines? Postcards? No, he says. He saw it in the movies.

Left: John Mauceri and the Hollywood Bowl Orchestra in one of their regular concert tributes to the music of Hollywood

Right: Conductor John Green.

Midnight at the Oasis: Jazz

BY GENE LEES

A s a young man growing up in Canada, my first impression of the Hollywood Bowl came in a 1945 movie called *Anchors Aweigh*, which starred Gene Kelly and Frank Sinatra. They played two sailors on leave who are trying to get a break for an aspiring singer played by Kathryn Grayson. To do this, they connive to introduce her to pianist José Iturbi — played by José Iturbi — and of course they do so and all ends happily. In real life, Grayson did sing at the Bowl in 1946 and several times thereafter. Iturbi was a regular there for years, both as conductor and as pianist.

Iturbi in those days was presented in movies as a great classical pianist who now and then deigned to play boogie-woogie. This was to show his common touch, this cheerful little man from Spain, and it was sort of a joke. But more significantly, those excursions into boogie by a concert pianist revealed the condescension toward jazz and its collateral branches endemic in respectable musical society in those days.

To be sure, jazz had been performed at Carnegie Hall by Benny Goodman on January 16, 1938, in what is still often labeled the first jazz concert, although it wasn't. W. C. Handy had presented a huge concert of black music at Carnegie ten years before that, and a concert of swing music, featuring Artie Shaw, Bunny Berigan, and Teddy Wilson, among others, was staged at the Imperial Theatre in May 1936. In terms of stature and publicity value, the Hollywood Bowl was already the West Coast equivalent of Carnegie Hall, and Goodman followed his Carnegie appearance with a special non-subscription concert at the Bowl in 1939. But jazz was still a long way from its present recognition as a major art form.

In *Anchors Aweigh*, Sinatra was cast as a naive boob from Brooklyn. But in reality, he was already recognized by many listeners as a sophisticated and revolutionary artist who had brought to the interpretation of classic American songs the perception, intelligence, and dignity they deserved. Furthermore, he had played the Hollywood Bowl in 1943, two years before that movie was released, in a performance greeted by an adoring legion of bobby-soxers and rather more frostily by conservatives who felt Bowl traditions were being demeaned in some fashion. Sinatra seems to have been the first jazz performer to play the Bowl at a regular subscription concert.

Ella Fitzgerald.

Above: Mel Tormé rehearses.
Right: George Shearing and
John Williams in concert.

There are, of course, purists who would say Sinatra was not a jazz artist. But for years he won in the favorite-singer category in such jazz magazines as *Down Beat* and *Metronome*, and in 1956, when the late Leonard Feather (for many years a regular at the Bowl as a jazz critic for the *Los Angeles Times*) polled jazz musicians, an overwhelming majority of them, including Lester Young and Nat Cole, named Sinatra their favorite male singer. And so Sinatra certainly belongs in the history of jazz at the Hollywood Bowl.

But jazz remained a rare commodity at the Bowl in the 1940s. Though the early '40s were the height of the big band era, none of the major bands appeared there then. To be sure, they had thousands of other locations to play throughout North America, and in any case what they played still was looked on as appropriate for dance halls, not concerts. By the mid-1940s, Stan Kenton was insisting on its legitimacy as concert music, to be heard from seats in auditoriums.

In 1945, Sinatra again appeared at the Bowl, and the next year, the Bowl's 25th season, Sinatra, Lena Horne, and Jo Stafford were heard there. Through the rest of the '40s, real instrumental jazz remained conspicuous by its absence, excepting a special performance by Duke Ellington and His Orchestra in 1947, benefiting the building fund of the Southeast Youth Center, and Stan Kenton the following season, also non-subscription. Popular singers — among them Lanny Ross, Helen Forrest, Johnny Mercer, and Gordon MacRae — became slightly more frequent performers, for the obvious reason that singers had a repertory which they could present with an orchestra.

In 1953, Peggy Lee made her debut appearance at the Bowl. "I was terrified," she says, but she conquered her fear to become one of the Bowl's enduringly popular artists. She also did one of the first television shows ever shot at the Bowl. "I had on this beautiful yellow gown that was, to say the least, form-fitting," she remembers. "It was fine until the lights hit it in rehearsal. Then I looked nude. I sent home for another gown, and this one had stripes on it. So from looking nude I went to looking like a leopard."

The Bowl heard Eddie Fisher, Tony Martin, Ethel Merman, and Nat "King" Cole in 1954. That same year, Benny Goodman made a subscription concert appearance, playing the Weber Clarinet Concerto with the Los Angeles Philharmonic under Leroy Anderson. He finished the program with his trio: himself, Teddy Wilson on piano, and Louie Bellson on drums. Goodman returned in 1960 and '63.

Finally, in 1956, Ella Fitzgerald, the very archetype of a jazz singer, performed there with Louis Armstrong, one of the founding giants of jazz. Their performances are the cornerstone of a double album from Verve, "Jazz at the Hollywood Bowl," issued in 1956. Other artists on the recording include Art Tatum and the Oscar Peterson Trio, who also appeared at the Bowl that summer.

By then, Cole was becoming an annual regular. Fitzgerald and Armstrong were back in 1957, along with the Oscar Peterson Trio, Harry "Sweets" Edison, and the Gerry Mulligan Quartet — the Jazz at the Philharmonic troupe of traveling players. Jazz at the Philharmonic — named for

Michael Tilson Thomas and Miss Peggy Lee.

Henry Mancini began appearing at the Bowl in 1962.

Left: Carmen McRae.

Right: Dave Brubeck.

Philharmonic Auditorium in Los Angeles, the home of the Los Angeles Philharmonic for many years — was the work of impresario Norman Granz, who was proving the validity of jazz as a concert music with his increasingly successful tours. It was Granz who had brought Fitzgerald and company to the Bowl in 1956.

Granz was a young film editor when he began presenting jazz performers in Los Angeles clubs. Then, on the afternoon of July 2, 1944, he presented Nat Cole, Buddy Rich, Benny Carter, and others at Philharmonic Hall to raise money for what was called "The Sleepy Lagoon Defense Fund." The fund was used to defend Mexican-American young men arrested on questionable grounds during the so-called "Zoot Suit Riots." The concert was so successful that Granz launched a series of touring concerts titled Jazz at the Philharmonic, which changed the way jazz was presented forever and enabled Granz to launch a series of successful record labels, including Norgran, Clef, Verve, and Pablo.

One of his main stars was Ella Fitzgerald. He not only presented her, he became her manager, and guided her career to the point of making her a wealthy woman. By 1958 she was bigger than she had ever been and she was back at the Bowl. Anita O'Day and Joe Williams turned up on the roster, and that year there was a special appearance by the Count Basie Orchestra.

Perhaps the most significant jazz event at the Bowl of the mid-'50s that was not singer-centered was the "Jazz Symposium" held in 1955 as part of Leonard Bernstein's Festival of the Americas. Bernstein moderated a discussion with André Previn and writers Leonard Feather and Ralph Gleason. Performing sets as part of this symposium were Dave Brubeck with his quartet, Buddy de Franco and his quartet, Billie Holiday, Pete Kelly and His Big Seven, alto saxophonist Lee Konitz,

André Previn as a piano soloist, Shorty Rogers and His Giants with drummer Shelly Manne, and Cal Tjader with his Afro-Cuban group.

In 1959 the first Los Angeles Jazz Festival was a two-day post-season event in October, featuring Count Basie, Bobby Darin, George Shearing, Sarah Vaughan, Shorty Rogers, Nina Simone, the Hi-Lo's, and Cal Tjader. A month earlier, the 12th annual Dixieland Jubilee was held at the Bowl, with Louis Armstrong headlining a bill that also listed Mort Sahl, the Pete Kelly Seven, the Firehouse Five Plus Two, and the Teddy Buckner Band.

Louis Armstrong returned in 1961, but instrumental jazz remained relatively rare. The Tommy Dorsey Orchestra played the Bowl in 1964 (with Helen Forrest in a return visit), and then, in 1965, the Miles Davis Quintet and the Gerry Mulligan Quartet — both well established as concert groups — played there. The next year Miles Davis came back with composer and arranger Gil Evans, collaborators on a series of brilliant albums for Columbia Records. In 1966, the Duke Ellington Orchestra returned to the Bowl, and the George Shearing Quintet appeared for the first time.

In 1967 the pace accelerated. Ella Fitzgerald appeared with the Ellington band, and Dizzy Gillespie, Stan Getz, Carmen McRae, Wes Montgomery, Sarah Vaughan, and Count Basie all played the Bowl. The next year Duke Ellington was back, but his was the only jazz group to appear that year. In 1969 and '70, the jazz action moved across the freeway to the Pilgrimage Theater (later the John Anson Ford Amphitheatre) for ambitious festivals.

In August 1972, Oscar Peterson returned, this time with composer and arranger Percy Faith. By then, pop, rock, and folk stars provided substantial parts of each season's programming. Attendance figures show that the pop acts generally outdrew the jazz shows by 2:1 margins or better, which may explain the relative paucity of jazz programming.

That began to change in June of 1973, when four of George Wein's Newport Jazz Festival concerts were presented. The last two performances outdrew most of the pop acts appearing at the Bowl. The next year, however, the only jazz at the Bowl was a Duke Ellington Memorial concert and a weekend of Cleo Laine with Henry Mancini conducting; Laine provided the only jazz presence in 1975 and 1976. Sarah Vaughan and Carmen McRae sang a concert under the baton of Calvin Simmons in 1977, and in 1978 Chuck Mangione played a night at the Bowl, captured live on an A&M recording released in 1979 as "An Evening of Magic."

Jazz fortunes improved dramatically in 1979, when George Wein produced the first Playboy Jazz Festival at the Bowl. On Friday, June 15, the attendance was reported as 12,243, while the figure for Saturday, June 16, was 16,437 — numbers on par with the leading pop acts. Attendance would remain at these levels through the 1980s and '90s. Because of this response, the Japanese consumer

Tito Puente and Pancho Sanchez.

Grover Washington, Jr.

electronics corporation JVC began to sponsor an annual contemporary jazz concert in 1985.

In 1980 Ernest Fleischmann introduced Jazz at the Bowl, a series of Wednesday night concerts produced by Wein's West Coast office. The artists for the first season included Chick Corea, Ray Brown, the L.A. Four, Mel Tormé, Carmen McRae, Joe Williams, Dave Brubeck, Bill Evans, George Shearing, and blues masters B.B. King, Muddy Waters, Big Joe Turner, and Big Mama Thornton.

In 1987, the two days of the Playboy Jazz Festival sold out completely, for a total of almost 36,000 persons. On some Wednesday night concerts, Ella Fitzgerald proved able to sell out the Bowl without a supporting act. The success of the Wein-produced weekend concerts was preserved on record with the 1984 release of Elektra's "In Performance at the Playboy Jazz Festival."

George Wein has been rightly called the Sol Hurok of jazz. Only Norman Granz, now retired, can be compared to him, and Granz never produced festivals. Wein was born in Boston on October 3, 1925, the son of a prominent physician. He studied piano with Margaret Chaloff, mother of baritone saxophone Serge Chaloff and one of the most distinguished piano teachers in America; she trained many major jazz pianists, and even established concert pianists would stop in Boston to consult with her. Later, Wein became fascinated by jazz piano, later studying with Teddy Wilson. He did pre-med studies at Boston University, intending to become a doctor, but by then he was playing piano with various groups and he eventually dropped medicine for music. He became nationally known for Storyville, a jazz club he opened in Boston.

In 1954 he produced the first of the Newport Jazz Festivals. It must be remembered that the very idea of a jazz festival was new. There had never been one before, and Newport (and Wein) helped establish jazz as a serious concert music. He continued to produce the Newport festivals, and in 1959 expanded his activities to produce (under the Newport name) festivals in French Lick, Indiana, as well as Toronto, Boston, and Europe.

In 1970, Wein moved the Newport Jazz Festival to New York, and expanded it to a ten-night event. As noted above, in 1973 he brought Newport to the Hollywood Bowl. In the summer of 1974, he established La Grande Parade du Jazz in Nice, France, and founded the New York Jazz Repertory Company.

He also continued to play piano, appearing as the leader of his Newport All-Stars. Wein is curiously self-deprecating about his own piano playing. He told one interviewer, "I reach a wall I can't go over in my playing. I'd have been a better player if I had studied more. The harmony and voicings just aren't there for me like they are for others. I wasn't a natural. I'd not have been the best."

Maybe. But he is nonetheless a very good jazz pianist, and this perhaps contributes to his keen sense of the talent of others.

"We do amazingly well in attendance at the Bowl," Wein says. "If you ask me why, I don't know. We have to take a fairly commercial approach to the music. In general, we try to keep the music at a certain level and it seems to be working.

"A lot of it has to do with the Bowl itself. I know very well that if I put the same concert on at another location in Los Angeles, it would draw less than half what it does at the Bowl. There are a lot of outdoor venues in the Los Angeles area, but you don't see any jazz playing there.

"The Bowl has a mystique about it. It also has an older audience, although we get a tremendous number of young people. The Playboy Festival is just an incredible happening," he says. "Who knows why? I've just been doing these things so many years. You fall into good habits and bad habits. I just have one philosophy: if nobody comes to my concerts, I'm not going to be giving any concerts. It's been a challenge and it continues to be a challenge. Of course, working with Darlene Chan is wonderful. Without her I'd have to break my neck on the West Coast."

"I've been with George since 1968," says Chan, senior vice president of Wein's Festival Productions, the parent organization of Wein's far-flung activities. Since she and Wein have been producing the Playboy Jazz Festival and Jazz at the Bowl, they have presented more than 30 groups a year there, a total of thousands of musicians.

The venue has become a very special place for the musicians involved. Mel Tormé, for example, has performed annually at the Bowl for 20 years, on the jazz series and in concerts with the Los Angeles Philharmonic, and would be happy to extend that streak indefinitely. "The Hollywood Bowl with its thousands of seats is one of the most intimate venues in which I appear," he says. "The ambience of the super enclosure is beyond belief. And for my part, I hope the relationship between yours truly and the Bowl never ends."

"It's beautiful to look at, from the outside and the inside," says jazz and classical trumpeter Wynton Marsalis, a frequent Bowl performer. "They have a great sound system and the people backstage are nice. As a performer, that's all you want."

Jazz now helps support more than just itself at the Bowl. The Los Angeles Philharmonic Association engaged Wein's company to produce Jazz at the Bowl. All proceeds go to the Association, and thus contribute to the funding of the Philharmonic and other activities at the Bowl. The Bowl performances in turn generate immense amounts of work for jazz musicians. "I think of it as art supporting art," Chan says.

Nor does Playboy retain profits from the Playboy Jazz Festival. The festival frequently has sold out all 17,900 seats of the Bowl, but not a penny of the proceeds goes to Playboy. "Whatever they make and more," Chan says, "goes to present free community concerts all during the month of May and June. We do one at Santa Monica College that draws over 10,000. We did one at Pasadena that drew over 20,000. They do a free small senior citizens concert in Watts. They've been doing that for many years.

"Since we were selling out at the Bowl," Chan continues, "not everybody could attend the festival. And not everybody could afford to come to the Bowl. So Hugh Hefner's game plan from day one was that any profits made would be used to bring jazz to the community."

The Bowl has known sad occasions as well as happy ones. Woody Herman and the Young Thundering Herd appeared there, on a bill with Mel Tormé and George Shearing, in August 1983. And then, on the evening of July 16, 1986, Herman and his band, along with some of the alumni from his earlier bands, performed in a special 50th Anniversary Celebration. Actually, his half-century anniversary as a bandleader wouldn't occur until November, but the July date was the only one available at the Bowl.

Clarinetist Richard Stoltzman was a guest on the program, performing the *Ebony*

Left: Bobby McFerrin and Chick Corea rehearse.
Right: Wynton Marsalis.

Los Lobos.

Concerto that Woody had commissioned from Igor Stravinsky in 1945 and premiered at Carnegie Hall on March 25, 1946.

Woody, in failing health, was no longer able to play it. He was penniless, having been hounded for 20 years by the Internal Revenue Service for a debt that was not his fault in the first place. Its agents frequently seized his box office receipts at the end of performances, and finally their pressures crumpled him. He would never appear at the Bowl again; he died of a symphony of ailments 16 months after that Bowl performance, on October 29, 1987.

According to Dave Brubeck, the Bowl is a challenging place to play. The immense distances, and the size of the audiences involved, make performing there a daunting matter. At one time, to make matters more difficult, there was a reflecting pool in front of the stage — almost a moat — and performers had to "throw" their work across it. "I was so glad when they got rid of the water," Brubeck says.

"I've played there so many times and in so many ways. The seating is 18,000, but we've done as much as 21,000 there with George Wein." (Listeners were scattered on the hill above the regular seating.) "The first time Barbra Streisand sang there, she followed me. I had never heard of her. Neither had the audience. She was trembling like a leaf backstage before she went on. Then she walked out and *killed* that crowd.

"Sammy Davis followed her," Brubeck continued, "and he presented every bit of his showmanship. He sang, he tap-danced, he played the drums, until he got the applause he wanted. But it wasn't easy, after Streisand. There was a cross on a hill that you could see from the stage. Sammy looked up and said, 'Do you think they're trying to tell me something?' He broke up the whole crowd.

"One of my sad memories of the Bowl involves Bill Evans. I did a concert there, three pianists — myself, George Shearing, and Bill. Afterwards, Bill's bass player came to my dressing room. He said that Bill asked him to say hello and to tell me that he wasn't feeling well and he had to leave immediately for San Francisco.

"That concert was the last time I ever saw Bill Evans." (The performance date was August 27, 1980; Evans died less than three weeks later, on September 15.)

Jazz today is firmly established throughout the world as a major art form, with thousands of high schools, colleges, and universities teaching it as a formal subject. It is now more than half a century since Gene Kelly and Frank Sinatra went bounding down the steps of the Bowl to buttonhole José Iturbi. Jazz has come a long, long way since Iturbi sat down to play a little boogie and lend it a small measure of respectability. And the Hollywood Bowl has played no small part in advancing the cause of this most American of musics.

THE ULTIMATE VENUE: ROCK AND POP

....

To get to Carnegie Hall, the old joke goes, practice, practice, practice. But for the elite group of top pop and rock artists who have performed at the Hollywood Bowl, getting to America's most venerable outdoor concert venue is more than a matter of practicing with relentless determination and endless perseverance. It is a reward — a sign of prestige and distinguished accomplishment — that only the very best have achieved.

"It's the ultimate venue," said keyboardist Ray Manzarek, who performed at the Bowl with The Doors in 1968.

"You have a feeling of having arrived," agreed 1971 Bowl performer James Taylor.

"I don't think there's another place in America that has the heart-shaking impact of the Hollywood Bowl," said Bonnie Raitt, who drew capacity crowds to her 1992 and 1994 Bowl shows. "It's a fantastic place to play, and it has so much history."

That history is formidable indeed, spanning a stylistic breadth nearly as rich and varied as pop music itself. No wonder the list of musicians to grace the Hollywood Bowl's stage reads like a Who's Who of popular music.

Although singers in the early years of the Bowl often included popular ballads on their programs, the list of pop artists in the modern sense begins with Frank Sinatra, who made his Bowl debut in 1943. He was followed in the 1950s by Nat "King" Cole, Bobby Darin, Ray Charles, Johnnie Ray, Mahalia Jackson, Sammy Davis Jr., and Little Richard. Then came The Beatles, Rolling Stones, Who, Buffalo Springfield, Ravi Shankar, Jackson Five, Grateful Dead, Aretha Franklin, Pink Floyd, Willie Nelson, Rod Stewart, Fleetwood Mac, Sting, Morrissey, Garth Brooks, Tom Petty, New Order, and Elton John, whose eight Bowl concerts in three decades is a record for a pop artist.

The list also includes more than a few superstars who are instantly identifiable by just their surnames — Dylan, Streisand, McCartney, Hendrix, Joplin, Zappa, Vandross, Ronstadt, Buffett, Connick, Houston, Iglesias, Santana, Manilow, Bolton.

The Beatles.

Nat "King" Cole.

And it's a list that encompasses nearly every contemporary musical style or hybrid: blues (B.B. King, Etta James, Buddy Guy); soul (Otis Redding, Sly & The Family Stone, Isaac Hayes); folk (Joan Baez, Arlo Guthrie, Josh White); country (Merle Haggard, Johnny Cash, Tex Ritter); progressive rock (Yes, Procol Harum, Emerson, Lake & Palmer); hard-rock and heavy-metal (Vanilla Fudge, Deep Purple, Black Sabbath); and soft-rock (the Association, the Carpenters, Seals & Croft).

Other idioms that have been showcased at the Hollywood Bowl include: psychedelia (Jefferson Airplane, Iron Butterfly, Soft Machine); roots-rock (The Band, Creedence Clearwater Revival, Los Lobos); jazz-rock (Chicago, Blood, Sweat & Tears); blues-rock (the Electric Flag, the Allman Brothers); folk-rock (Lovin' Spoonful, the Mamas and the Papas); funk (War, the Crusaders); New Wave (the Go-Gos, the Thompson Twins); country-rock (Stephen Stills & Manassas); dance-pop (Donna Summer); hip-hop (P.M. Dawn); Nigerian juju music (King Sunny Ade); and even so-called "shock"-rock (Alice Cooper, whose 1972 concert included enough special effects for a Boris Karloff tribute).

"The Hollywood Bowl is such a classic music place, and it has such a great mystique," said former Knack drummer Bruce Geary, a Los Angeles native who attended many of the ground-breaking pop concerts at the Bowl in the 1960s. "I wish I could say I performed there, but that has eluded me. It has such an importance in the history of Los Angeles — and the history of music."

So far as can be determined, twangy guitar-slinger Duane Eddy holds the distinction of being the first bona fide rocker to appear at the Bowl. Eddy's 1958 performance coincided with the first of several Dick Clark-produced revues at the Bowl, which subsequently hosted everyone from rockabilly pioneer Dorsey Burnette, Santo & Johnny, and short-lived teen pop idol Bobby Rydell, to surf-rock vocal duo Jan & Dean and "Beach Blanket Bingo" stars Frankie Avalon and Annette Funicello.

But the Hollywood Bowl and rock 'n' roll didn't really become synonymous until the mid-1964 arrival of The Beatles. It was an event that quickly became the stuff of legend.

With Beatlemania exploding across the land, the Fab Four's August 23 concert sold out in an instant and drew 18,000 frenzied fans. Together, they created a degree of hysteria so great it made the hyperactive bobby-soxers who attended Frank Sinatra's 1943 Bowl debut seem almost sedate by comparison.

"The management knew they would have a panic situation, so they hired a Brinks armored truck to bring The Beatles from their hotel and to take them back," said Hollywood Bowl Museum director Carol Merrill-Mirsky.

"I remember that quite vividly," added "Uncle" Max Foster, who has worked at the Hollywood Bowl box office since 1938 and is now its assistant treasurer. "The young people were walking on top of cars when The Beatles arrived, and some of the car roofs got crushed. Security and police were trying to stop them, but there were so many kids and they were so determined to get back-stage and see The Beatles step out of the armored truck. It was pandemonium. I haven't seen anything

like it before or since."

Los Angeles music photographer Heather Harris was only 12 when she attended The Beatles' Bowl debut. But it's a performance she remembers as clearly as yesterday.

"It was the event of the season if you were a kid," said Harris, who also attended The Beatles' two 1965 Bowl shows. "And it's a visual memory, because you didn't hear anything; the people screaming overpowered the band. It was also fun to see various music celebrities in the audience, like The Byrds, who were just as enthusiastic, although they didn't scream."

"The girls in the audience were so loud that it was like standing in a jet stream!" Geary recalled of the Mop Tops' second 1965 Bowl concert. "It was an amazing experience."

Twelve years later, in 1977, Capitol Records released "The Beatles At The Hollywood Bowl," an album featuring songs taken from the band's 1964 and 1965 Bowl performances. The album captures the excitement of the shows very well, less so the music that was played.

"I think that was the only time the sound was bad at the Bowl," said veteran Los Angeles rock radio host Rodney Bingenheimer, who cites The Beatles' 1964 Bowl gig as his first rock concert. "I understand that on the album they brought up the vocal and instrumental tracks in the mix, and tried to lower the screaming as much as they could."

Those screams returned (albeit not nearly as loud or frenzied) in 1993, when former Beatle Paul McCartney headlined an Earth Day benefit concert at the Bowl. "You look a bit different than

John and Bonnie Raitt.

the last time I was here," McCartney slyly told the capacity audience, after performing an exuberant version of The Beatles' "We Can Work It Out."

For the concert's finale of "Hey Jude," McCartney and his band were joined by ex-Beatles drummer Ringo Starr, k.d. lang, and fellow Earth Day concert performers Don Henley, Steve Miller, 10,000 Maniacs, P.M. Dawn, Bruce Cockburn, and Kenny Loggins.

The Beatles' Bowl concerts had both musical and commercial significance, and the number of rock and pop bookings grew in their wake. (In a curious coincidence, The Beatles' first Bowl appearance in 1964 came only nine days after a Bowl show by musical satirist Allan Sherman, of "I Hate The Beatles" fame.)

Bob Dylan and The Beach Boys both made their Bowl debuts in 1965, a year that also saw the venue host concerts by Johnny Mathis and Peter, Paul & Mary. The following year brought the return of The Beach Boys and the debuts of Sonny & Cher and the Rolling Stones.

"Dylan got a few obligatory boos because he was playing with his first electric band," recalled Geary. "But for the most part, it was a very appreciative audience."

As rock became the dominant sound of the decade, radio stations and record stores in the Los Angeles area began sponsoring concerts at the Bowl. One of the most memorable came in November of 1967, when the White Front record store chain provided free Bowl tickets for its "Festival of Music" to customers who bought any album on the Decca or Reprise label.

"For spending $2.50 each on an album at White Front, my friend and I got second-row center box seats," said noted Los Angeles music and spoken-word producer Harvey Kubernik. "We got to see the Association, Who, Eric Burdon's New Animals, Sopwith Camel, the Sunshine Co., and the Everly Brothers. As I recall, the Bowl wasn't very user-friendly for rock 'n' roll at the time and did not welcome longhaired rock fans. But because of that Who concert, a lot of other groups started playing there."

Those groups included, in 1968, The Doors and the Jimi Hendrix Experience. Both concerts were memorable, although for distinctly different reasons. For their part, The Doors wanted to be heard "up over the hill, as far away as Grauman's Chinese Theater on Hollywood Boulevard," recalled keyboardist Manzarek.

The Doors, whose Bowl show was taped and filmed for subsequent album and video release, asked the company that made its sound gear to provide every available amplifier for the band's July 5 Bowl concert. The company responded with 60 amplifiers, and the band had 30 set up on either side of the stage. Singer Jim Morrison's vocal microphone was hooked directly into the Bowl's house P.A. system.

"This was where Stravinsky and all these greats had conducted, so to step on that stage was like playing Carnegie Hall," Manzarek said. "Unfortunately, about a half hour before we went on, a man came up to us with a decibel meter. He said: 'I'm sitting next to the sound man at the mixing board, and if you go over 110 decibels, we're pulling the plug.' And we looked at each other and said:

'Oh, s—!' So, for all the trouble we went to, we were reduced to playing with our usual amplification.

"It looked great — what a look! — but all the amps were turned off, except for two for the guitar, two for my keyboard bass, and two for my organ."

Manzarek chuckled when asked if the Doors' audience, which included four of the five Rolling Stones, was aware of this aural subterfuge. "You know what?" he replied. "Don't tell them. That's our little secret. They never knew." Indeed, they didn't. "I was there and I wasn't aware of it," acknowledged Geary. "But it looked ridiculous, this wall of amps, and they were playing loud regardless. Funnily enough, when I saw Jimi Hendrix at the Bowl, he had a wall of amps and they were all on. It was so loud that the material that covers the amps was peeling and ripping from the strain of the volume. He had something like ten amps and so did Noel (Redding, Hendrix's bassist).

"Hendrix was blowing amps up left and right, and it was the loudest show I saw at the Bowl — with the exception of the audience at the Beatles' show!"

Electric guitar master Hendrix's 1968 concert was actually his second show at the Bowl. The first was a 1967 concert, opening for the Mamas and the Papas, in front of a decidedly unappreciative audience. "We died a death," bassist Redding would later say of that performance.

But by 1968 Hendrix was himself a major star, and his Bowl concert drew a near-capacity crowd. Some fans reacted to his galvanizing music with almost electrifying results — literally — when they swarmed into the four-foot-deep pool of water that separated the stage from the audience.

"When Hendrix started playing 'Purple Haze,' about 2,500 people rushed down to the front," Geary recounted. "It got so crazy that I got pushed into the pool, and my camera was ruined. There must've been 100 or more people in the water.

"At one point, someone was tugging on a microphone cord, and the microphone nearly fell in the water. Just as it was falling, Hendrix stopped it with his foot. I believe everyone would've been electrocuted, so he saved our lives. There was a lot of water on stage, and it was total chaos."

Hendrix was not the only rock performer at the Bowl whose music inspired fans to jump into the pool, which was removed in 1970. But water, in the form of rain, played a dramatic role in a number of other Bowl concerts over the years, few more memorable than those by pop diva Judy Garland in 1946 and hippie troubadour Donovan in 1968.

"She was simply marvelous," "Uncle" Max Foster recalled of Garland. "I've never seen so many celebrities at the Bowl — all of our lower boxes were filled with movie stars. But the amazing thing was how she could hold an audience. As she sang, it began to sprinkle and then to rain, but not a soul left. And I've never heard her better than that night."

At one point, Garland strode across a temporary catwalk jutting out from the front of the stage. She proceeded to sing with no protection from the rain whatsoever, a bravura action that earned her an especially warm ovation from the drenched crowd. But in the case of Donovan some 22 years later, the rain was short-lived, thanks to a stroke of cosmic serendipity.

When it began sprinkling during his concert, the Scottish singer-songwriter told the 17,000-plus members of his audience that, together, they could stop the rain simply by

Jimi Hendrix.

thinking it away. A few moments later, the rain stopped, and the remainder of the show took place under dry skies. Donovan can be heard relating this mind-over-water-episode on his "In Concert" album, which was recorded the following week at the Anaheim Convention Center.

As the late 1960s gave way to the early 1970s, rock and pop became firmly entrenched as a main course on the Bowl's musical menu. At the same time, the programming became more adventurous — if not always for the better.

In 1970, for example, a novel concert called "From Bach to the Blues" featured the unlikely pairing of classical pianist Lorin Hollander and the Los Angeles Philharmonic with deep-voiced soul singer Isaac Hayes. Two weeks later, the Philharmonic, conducted by Lawrence Foster, teamed with English hard-rock band Deep Purple, then touring to promote its portentous "Concerto for Group and Orchestra" album.

In 1972, a concert by the highly theatrical rock band Alice Cooper became the first and (to date) last at the Bowl to utilize a helicopter, which dropped free concert souvenirs onto the crowd below. The "souvenirs" in question were thousands of the same paper panties that adorned Cooper's then-current album, "School's Out." They were dropped from the helicopter as the singer and his band performed the album's anthemic title track. Mock high school diplomas were also given to the audience.

Alas, inaccurate navigation and shifting wind currents resulted in a fair number of those panties instead landing in the yards of nearby residents, who were none too pleased. "We got angry calls about that from our neighbors," said Mark Ferber, an usher at the Cooper concert who is now the Bowl's special events manager and production supervisor. "We were not advised that the helicopter was going to fly over."

The same 1972 season also brought English progressive rock band Pink Floyd to the Bowl. The quartet, whose landmark "Dark Side of the Moon" album would not be released until the following year, decided to live up to its name — literally. All of the stage lights and spotlights used for its Bowl concert were pink, as were the lights throughout the seating area. So were all of the lights outside the venue, putting the Bowl in the pink at least for one night.

As the number of rock and pop concerts at the Bowl increased in the 1970s, so did complaints from area residents about noise and traffic problems. Matters came to a head following shootings at Bowl concerts featuring Aretha Franklin in 1974 and Earth, Wind & Fire in 1975.

The seemingly less than coincidental result of these incidents was that no pop or rock concerts were held at the Bowl in 1976, and just two in 1977. This dry spell continued until 1982, when Elton John performed three concerts at the Bowl, where he had first appeared in 1973. The following six years found the venue almost bereft of pop and rock attractions, until John returned for three more shows in 1988.

But a real turnaround didn't come until 1992, when the Bowl hosted triumphant performances by Paul Simon and Sting, whose concert celebrated his 40th birthday and featured a brief on-stage reunion with guitarist Andy Summers, Sting's former band mate from The Police. Simon's and Sting's shows were the direct result of an exclusive, long-term contract that was signed in 1991 between the Los Angeles Philharmonic, San Diego's Bill Silva Presents, and Andy Hewitt, Silva's Los Angeles partner for all rock and pop shows at the Bowl.

Silva and Hewitt have since brought some of the biggest stars in contemporary music to the Bowl, in the process helping to re-establish it as one of the most prestigious venues for pop and rock in the nation.

Performers since 1992 include: Bonnie Raitt; Garth Brooks (who performed with John Mauceri and the Hollywood Bowl Orchestra); Whitney Houston; Rubén Blades; Harry Connick Jr.; José Luis Rodríguez; Morrissey; Michael Bolton; Celia Cruz; New Order; the Gipsy Kings; Linda Ronstadt: Tito Puente; Jimmy Buffett; Amy Grant; Tom Petty; the Moody Blues; and Elton John, whose two 1995 Bowl concerts were a highlight of the season.

To demonstrate just how special they consider the Bowl to be, Silva and Hewitt present every

artist they book to perform there with commemorative crystal bowls. These are replicas of the bowls Capitol Records presented to The Beatles after the Fab Four's first Bowl show in 1964, and include the Bowl's logo, the name of the artist, and the date of their concert.

"To Andy and me, the Bowl is a crown jewel, and we were dumbfounded and elated that we were handed the opportunity to bring shows there," said Silva, who has been friends with Hewitt since 1981.

"Basically, it was an overlooked venue to most rock promoters," added Hewitt. "It was perceived as a place that had great difficulties, and we made the commitment to deal with those issues and take the Bowl to the next level — which we've been able to do."

The difficulties Silva and Hewitt faced included the noise and traffic problems that had long prompted complaints from area residents. No less daunting was the narrow window of opportunity to present artists at the Bowl, whose first priority is to accommodate the Los Angeles Philharmonic, the Hollywood Bowl Orchestra, the Playboy Jazz Festival (which, in 1995, celebrated its 16th anniversary), and an annual series of jazz concerts.

"Plus, we were coming in on the heels of an alternative-rock concert series held at a smaller theater across the freeway from the Bowl," said Silva. "So the neighbors were understandably up in arms when they heard a pop promoter was coming in to the Bowl, and they protested and tried to stop us."

In response, an advisory committee was formed, consisting of residents, county government representatives, and Bowl management. The two promoters subsequently instituted a number of policies, including special promotion of the Bowl's park-and-ride program to curtail traffic, ensuring that performers adhered to the Bowl's curfew, and employing roving "hot teams" to respond to neighborhood complaints within a matter of minutes.

They also established a telephone hotline for area residents to call in the event of problems, hired extra security guards to patrol outside the Bowl, and won a court injunction to prevent counterfeit T-shirt vendors from disrupting pedestrian and auto traffic in the Bowl area. And they have avoided booking styles of music that might prove incompatible with the Bowl, such as heavy metal or hardcore punk.

"The Bowl is a special place and it needs special attention," said Hewitt, whose first visit to the venue was as a child to see Sonny & Cher in 1966. "It was always my favorite venue, long before I became a rock promoter, and Bill and I are very conscientious about whom we book. We really work with superstars."

Silva agreed, adding: "We're looking for world-class entertainers who, when paired with the Bowl, make for a great evening — and a great statement. I remember how happy Bonnie Raitt was after she performed at the Bowl in 1992, and how she couldn't wait to come back. That made me feel great." Raitt holds the distinction of being the only pop star, male or female, whose Bowl concerts have featured guest appearances by a famous namesake who had performed at the Bowl years earlier. "When I was a young girl, my dad sang at the Bowl for Easter sunrise services," said Raitt, referring to her father, Broadway musical star John Raitt. "To reach the point where I could headline at the Bowl, and be able to bring my dad out to sing with me, was absolutely a lifetime dream come true."

Concerned that her fans might not be able to see and hear her adequately from the rear of the Bowl, which is 445 feet from the stage, Raitt had a giant video screen erected on top of the stage and provided extra audio equipment to control sound dispersal. "Bonnie brought in some sound delay towers, and so did Sting, but now the Bowl has a new sound system with its own delay system," said Steve Redfearn — former vice president for Bill Silva Presents — who oversaw production of pop and rock concerts at the Bowl from 1992 through 1995.

"It's an older venue and wasn't built for rock 'n' roll, so you have to make adjustments. But that's one reason Bowl performances are usually spectacular — because it's so special. There are other venues in the U.S. that are beautiful, but the feeling at the Bowl is unique."

Rock and pop shows at the Bowl 30 and even 20 years ago were relatively simple affairs that required minimal production. But in the high-tech, razzle-dazzle '90s, sophisticated stage sets have become the norm. And some of them are simply too large to be accommodated on the Bowl's stage, which measures 90 feet across.

Fortunately, the Bowl's panoramic, tree-lined setting provides a stunning backdrop no amount of special effects can match. The unique aesthetic qualities of the Bowl have made it the subject of several songs. They range from actor Robert Clary's seldom-heard "In the 88th Row of the Hollywood Bowl," which was released in the mid-1950s, to Paul McCartney's "Rock Show," released in the mid-1970s, which includes the refrain: "Rock show! Hollywood Bowl!" And historic live albums or videos have been made at Bowl concerts by artists as varied as The Beatles, the English comedy troupe Monty Python's Flying Circus, and The Doors (whose film crew included a young cameraman by the name of Harrison Ford).

Happily, with each new year, the Bowl's musical legacy can only grow greater, as a few more top artists make the grade and perform at what many pop and rock stars consider one of the supreme concert venues anywhere.

"When you play the Hollywood Bowl," said singer-songwriter James Taylor, "you have a feeling — like at Carnegie Hall or the Royal Albert Hall in London — that you are playing in a major place, a place that has a lot of weight and is an important part of musical history. You have a feeling of having arrived."

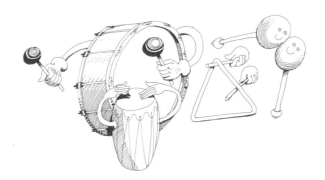

Elton John, 1995.

Michael Rabin
The Magic Bow
The Hollywood Bowl Symphony Orchestra
conducted by **Felix Slatkin**

PAGANINI-KREISLER: MOTO PERPETUO / KREISLER: THE OLD REFRAIN / RIMSKY-KORSAKOV-HEIFETZ: FLIGHT OF THE BUMBLE BEE / SAINT-SAENS: INTRODUCTION AND RONDO CAPRICCIOSO / KREISLER: CAPRICE VIENNOIS / DINICU-HEIFETZ: HORA STACCATO / MASSENET: MEDITATION FROM THAIS / SARASATE: ZIGEUNERWEISEN

THE BOWL ON RECORD

BY DENNIS BADE

The very first time might very well have been the last, considering the difficulties involved. In the summer of 1928 the first recordings were made on the stage of the Hollywood Bowl, with the British conductor Eugene Goossens at the helm of what was described on the labels of the six 12-inch Victor discs as the "Hollywood Bowl Orchestra." The collection of "typical" Bowl repertory included Dvořák's *Carnival* Overture and a suite from Tchaikovsky's *Sleeping Beauty*, as well as excerpts from Falla's *El amor brujo* and from Berlioz' *Symphonie fantastique*. The only slightly esoteric element in "A Hollywood Bowl Concert" was an orchestration (by Alfredo Casella) of Balakirev's finger-busting piano showpiece *Islamey*.

As the conductor, who had made his Bowl debut in 1926, relates the story in his autobiography (*Overture and Beginners*; London, 1951), "...These, I believe were the first open-air recordings ever made by a symphony orchestra, and turned out amazingly well. The faint sound of a high-flying aeroplane may be discerned by experts in the slow section of Dvořák's *Carnaval* [sic] *Overture*; this novel effect, though detected by the sound engineers during the orchestral recording, I do not consider too much of an anachronistic blemish to warrant condemning the record; nor indeed, is it really audible."

Writing some 20 years earlier, in an article for *The Gramophone* magazine of August 1930, Goossens had somewhat more to say about the matter. "Atmospheric conditions, and the fact that the microphone, placed about fifteen feet away from the platform, would inevitably have caught every movement and whisper of the public, obliged us to record for the gramophone in the mornings when the Bowl was empty. Even so, we discovered that an open-air studio had its disadvantages.

"Several of the first recordings were 'killed' by a summer breeze wafting across the Bowl and deflecting the sound from the microphone so that the music on the record suddenly faded in the most disconcerting manner. At first, too, we were puzzled by sounds like gunshots peppering the records here and there until experiment disclosed that the slightest crackle of turning pages had been enormously magnified by some curious atmospheric trick. And one of our finest efforts was completely ruined by an aeroplane which skimmed noisily overhead providing a gratuitous obbligato to Dvořák's *Carnival Overture*....

"The success of this experiment, carried out with a portable recording apparatus specially brought from New York, suggests that outdoor recordings might be attempted on a much larger scale now that electrical methods have eliminated the necessity for artists' working in studios fitted with a fixed apparatus. But for reproducing the utmost resonance and brilliance of orchestral playing, there is little doubt that the echo in an empty concert hall gives the most satisfactory results."

Future recordings by various instrumental aggregations carrying the Hollywood Bowl label would be made in more conventional studio surroundings scattered around the Los Angeles area, including a scoring stage at Republic Pictures (later CBS, later MTM, still later Todd-AO) in Studio City, a soundstage at the Samuel Goldwyn Studios (later Warner Hollywood) on Santa Monica Boulevard, one of the large studios at the Capitol Records tower in Hollywood, and the venerable scoring stage at MGM Studios (now Sony Pictures) in Culver City.

The engagement of the dashing and ever-marketable Leopold Stokowski as music director of a newly organized Hollywood Bowl Symphony led to a series of significant, but long-neglected, recordings for RCA Victor's Red Seal label which began in 1945 and included such varied repertory as Virgil Thomson's film score for *The Plow That Broke the Plains* (on two 12-inch discs), the Brahms Symphony No. 1, and Tchaikovsky's *Pathétique* Symphony (on six shellac records) and *Marche slave* (one record). In *Saturday Review*, Edward Tatnall Canby wrote about the sound quality of the Thomson release: "A splendid, wide-range recording...surpasses anything Victor has done this year... fine orchestral color, great clarity." The Thomson recording has been reissued on an RCA Gold Seal CD, along with the composer's abridged version of his *Four Saints in Three Acts*. In 1947, when Stokowski's Hollywood Bowl Symphony recording of Falla's *El amor brujo*, with the young American mezzo Nan Merriman (born 1920), was released just months after the death of the composer, it was heralded as a suitable memorial to "a great spirit in contemporary music." The two Tchaikovsky recordings were later reissued on Camden-label LPs by RCA Victor.

After Stokowski left his post at the Hollywood Bowl, he went on to become music director of the Houston Symphony. When he returned to conduct at the Bowl in August 1955, he performed two scores which he was soon to record for Capitol Records, not in Hollywood, but in Houston — Glière's *Ilya Murometz* and Orff's *Carmina Burana*. In August 1956, however, he did conduct a major work at the Bowl which was recorded with the Los Angeles Philharmonic for Capitol. It was Holst's grandiose suite, *The Planets*, and the recording was re-released by EMI Classics in 1994. Other music on that 1956 concert, which included Prokofiev's audacious *Scythian Suite*, did not make it into the studio.

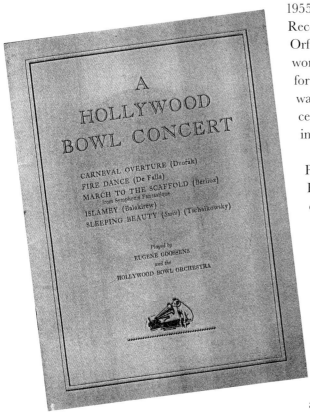

John Barnett, associate conductor of the Los Angeles Philharmonic from 1946 to 1958, became music director for the Hollywood Bowl Association as of the 1953 season. He conducted some of the early recordings (e.g., "Starlight Encores") under a productive contract with Capitol Records, but it was another American conductor whose sense of showmanship and sheer musical energy would contribute to one of the great success stories in recording history.

When Carmen Dragon made his Bowl debut in July 1950, the 35-year-old California native was already nationally popular as the conductor and host of several cross-country radio broadcasts, including the "Railroad Hour" and "Starlight Concert" (on NBC). During the next decade, he would make a long string of LPs with an ensemble which was known (for recording purposes) as the Hollywood Bowl Symphony Orchestra, although concert programs also listed it as the Hollywood Bowl "Pops" Orchestra or simply the Hollywood

Leopold Stokowski.

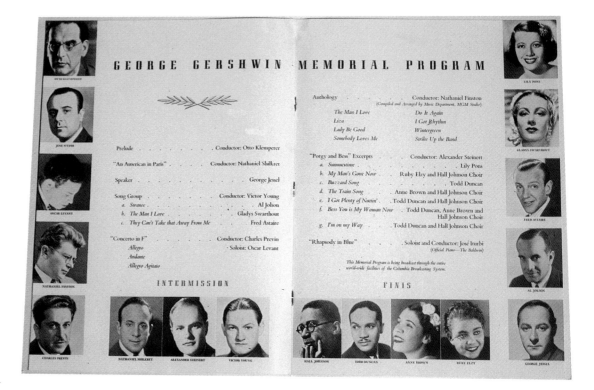

This memorial concert was held in 1937, the year of Gershwin's death. Performers included Lily Pons, Fred Astaire, Al Jolson, George Jessel, Ruby Elzy, Oscar Levant, and Otto Klemperer. Gershwin's music was always popular at the Bowl although he never performed there.

Bowl Orchestra (not to be confused with John Mauceri's Hollywood Bowl Orchestra of the 1990s). These albums often had fanciful titles to lure the buyer, such as "Fiesta!", "Chopin by Starlight," La Danza!," and "Gypsy!." In the 1960 Bowl program magazine, Capitol Records advertised Dragon's newest recordings, "Americana!", "A Concert Gala," a Stephen Foster collection, and "Tempo español."

It was Dragon's effervescent arrangements and repertory choices as much as the performances themselves which made these albums such hits with record buyers. Some purists were less than enchanted by the regularity with which original scores were tampered with for these recordings. In the program notes for a Saturday concert in August 1960, these startling lines appear: "In Mr. Dragon's arrangements [of waltzes from *The Gypsy Baron*], the limited original orchestrations for theater ensemble have been expanded for full symphony orchestra, and embellished with counter-melodies and obbligatos."

Carmen Dragon was not alone in the Hollywood Bowl Symphony Orchestra's success with the record-buying public. In the 1950s and the early 1960s, Felix Slatkin (leader of the Hollywood String Quartet and father of conductor Leonard Slatkin), Alfred Newman (head of the music department at 20th Century Fox), and Miklós Rózsa (composer of Oscar-winning motion picture scores including *Spellbound* and *Ben-Hur*) made recordings with the Hollywood Bowl Symphony Orchestra. As with the Carmen Dragon LPs, the repertory was chosen to reflect national styles or groups of similarly structured works ("Overture!", "Marche!", "Nocturne," "España," "Starlight Waltzes," etc.). In October 1995 a compilation of five compact discs issued by EMI Classics assembled much of the best material from the old Capitol catalog of recordings by the Hollywood Bowl Symphony Orchestra.

A favorite Bowl pianist who figured heavily in the recordings of the 1950s and '60s was Leonard Pennario. According to a biographical sketch in the August 1952 Hollywood Bowl program, Pennario had made his Los Angeles Philharmonic debut with music director Otto Klemperer conducting; the pianist was then still in high school, and the concert was one of the Philharmonic's Symphonies For Youth. It was on his 19th birthday, in July 1943, that Private Pennario played his first

Carmen Dragon, Leonard
Pennario.

concert at the Bowl. In addition to his recordings of Addinsell, Gershwin, and other "pops" repertory
with the Hollywood Bowl Symphony (in such collections as "Concertos Under the Stars" and
"Rhapsody Under the Stars"), Pennario recorded standard concerto fare with the Los Angeles
Philharmonic, including works by Grieg, Rachmaninoff, and Tchaikovsky. Several of those recordings
were reissued in 1995 by EMI Classics on compact discs bearing the Seraphim label.

In the Bowl program book's 1953 recording notes column, writer Fred Stern reports
that the gifted 17-year-old American violinist Michael Rabin has made his first
recording ("Michael Rabin Plays") for Columbia Records. In the program
for the second week of August 1954, a rather goofy-looking Rabin is pictured along with the Los Angeles Philharmonic's guest conductor that
week, a serene Georg Solti (at age 41); both Rabin and Solti were making
their Bowl debuts. Rabin later recorded with the Hollywood Bowl
Symphony and Felix Slatkin in a celebrated collaboration, "The Magic
Bow," issued by Capitol in 1960. All of the Capitol recordings he made have
been reissued in a set of six compact discs from EMI Classics.

The Los Angeles Philharmonic's music director between 1962 and
1978, Zubin Mehta, was only 25 years old when he made his Bowl debut in
August 1961. He conducted frequently at the Bowl, of course, and continues to
do so, but he made one recording which grew out of the first laser show at the
Bowl in November 1977. The London LP which resulted offered suites from the John Williams scores
for *Star Wars* and *Close Encounters of the Third Kind*. Even without the lasers, the recording was a success,
although it did turn out to be Mehta's last season as music director of the Philharmonic.

Forty-three years after Stokowski's short-lived Hollywood Bowl Symphony Orchestra was
disbanded, a new ensemble was established in 1991, the Hollywood Bowl Orchestra, under the direction of John Mauceri. The formation of the orchestra was directly linked to a recording contract with
Philips Classics, which had lost its lucrative Boston Pops Orchestra and conductor John Williams to

CBS/Sony Classical. Bernstein protégé Mauceri was selected to ensure a distinctive personality for the ensemble, which would explore the legacy of Hollywood music and provide relief for weary Philharmonic musicians by taking over most of the weekend concerts during the summer season.

"Let's not forget how ambitious it was to create an orchestra in the economic climate of the 1990s," comments Anne Parsons, who was brought to Los Angles to manage the Orchestra as well as the Summer Festival. "We had unprecedented support from a record company who committed to the creation of 15 CDs before the Orchestra had ever collected itself to play a note! In fact, our first gathering was in the very recording studio (MGM, now Sony) where so much of the music we record was first performed."

Mauceri and the Orchestra recorded "Hollywood Dreams" in February 1991, so that the CD would be available for sale in time for the Orchestra's first public performances at the 1991 Independence Day fireworks concerts. Their second CD that year was "The Gershwins in Hollywood," featuring vocalists Patti Austin and Gregory Hines. Both releases quickly climbed the charts, and the Gershwin CD went on to win Germany's highest recording award, the Deutsche Schallplattenpreis. By the end of their first year, John Mauceri and the Hollywood Bowl Orchestra had managed to complete three recordings, perform numerous Bowl concerts, and tour Japan, ringing in the New Year with performances in Osaka and Tokyo.

In short order, the Philips catalog grew to include new souvenirs of one of the most popular Bowl traditions, entire evenings devoted to great American songwriters: "Opening Night, the Complete Overtures of Rodgers and Hammerstein" and "Heat Wave: Patti LuPone Sings Irving Berlin." One Mauceri/Hollywood Bowl Orchestra project, *The King and I*, featured an all-star cast: Julie Andrews in the role of Anna and Ben Kingsley appearing as the King, with Lea Salonga (Broadway's "Miss Saigon"), Peabo Bryson, and Marilyn Horne, plus actors Roger Moore and Martin Sheen in special cameo appearances. In a typical Mauceri touch, the original orchestrations from the Academy Award-winning movie version of *The King and I* were resurrected and used for the recording.

In 1993, Mauceri and the Hollywood Bowl Orchestra released "American Classics" (including a newly edited reconstruction of Ellington's *Harlem* for jazz band and symphony orchestra) and "The Great Waltz" (a compilation ranging from Strauss, Ravel, and Prokofiev to Korngold, Steiner, Sondheim, and Loewe). 1994 saw the issue of an intriguing concept album, "Songs of the Earth — Twenty-Five Hours on the Planet" (with works by Debussy, Delius, and Nielsen, along with a Stokowski transcription of music from Wagner's *Tristan und Isolde)* and "Hollywood Nightmares," which included a "sonata for orchestra" arranged by Mauceri from Franz Waxman's score for *Sunset*

Heifetz, Piatigorsky, and Bernstein rehearse, 1963.

Gustav Holst's *Planets* is given special effects with this laser light show.

Boulevard and a new recording of an old Bowl favorite, Rózsa's *Spellbound Concerto*, with pianist Stephen Hough. In 1995, an all science-fiction collection, "Journey to the Stars," brought new performances of music by Bliss (*Things to Come*), Herrmann (*The Day the Earth Stood Still*), and Waxman (*The Bride of Frankenstein*), among others.

Bowl concerts were broadcast regularly for many years, and, beginning in 1944, the "Symphonies Under the Stars" were transcribed for broadcast over the Armed Forces Radio Service. For three years, "The Standard Hour" offered weekly concerts by the Hollywood Bowl Symphony (under Stokowski in 1945 and 1946, then in 1947 under a variety of conductors, from Antal Dorati and Vladimir Golschmann to Izler Solomon and William Steinberg). One issue of the 1950 Bowl program book announces that the NBC radio network would be recording and producing an hour-long Bowl program to be aired (everywhere *except* in Los Angeles) on Sunday afternoons.

In countries such as Italy, where copyright restrictions are less stringent, some broadcast recordings of Bowl concerts with artists such as Bruno Walter, Serge Koussevitzky, and Vladimir Horowitz have been released, but these discs are not authorized, either by the performing artists or by the musicians' union. One live concert which would have made a blockbuster recording was Sunday, September 1, 1963, when Leonard Bernstein and the New York Philharmonic were in residence and the soloists (in the Brahms Double Concerto) were Jascha Heifetz and Gregor Piatigorsky.

Few are the video mementos of Bowl performances. The music of Gershwin, a crowd-pleaser at the Bowl even though the composer himself never appeared there, figured in one of the rare video documents from the Bowl, with pianist Dudley Moore and conductor Michael Tilson Thomas in a 1981 salute to the composer. Shot during recording sessions at the Sony Pictures Studios, a one-hour documentary of "The Making of *The King and I*" was nominated for an Emmy and aired on PBS stations across the country in 1993. For something completely different, the inspired lunacy of Monty Python's Flying Circus was captured on film in performance at the Bowl in September 1980.

A 1963 post-season concert of film music with many celebrated composers conducting their own works was recorded and issued on LP by Columbia under the title "Music from Hollywood"; it has been reissued on a CD in the Legacy series. Pop music and jazz at the Bowl have spawned surprisingly few recordings. Exceptions include The Beatles (who appeared in 1964 and 1965) and The Doors (in 1968). Their dynamic Bowl performances are newly available on compact disc. Another treasurable highlight is a 2-LP Verve album recorded and issued in 1956, "Jazz at the Hollywood Bowl," with Ella Fitzgerald and other jazz giants (including Art Tatum and Louis Armstrong) in a Norman Granz extravaganza in the tradition of his famous Jazz at the Philharmonic events.

It is perhaps ironic that one of the world's great performance venues should have spawned such a legacy of recorded treasures; the very reason for the Hollywood Bowl's enduring success, and its place in the hearts of so many millions, is the unique opportunity it offers for an unequalled *live* performing experience, for artist and audience member alike. Recorded souvenirs are like postcards; the message is clear: "You shoulda been there!"

Prior to recording Franz Waxman's music for *The Bride of Frankenstein*, John Mauceri consults with the composer's son John Waxman, 1994..

What's a Performance Without an Audience?

BY ORRIN HOWARD

Most concertgoers who attend the Hollywood Bowl for the first time tend to be awed by the size and scope of that amazing piece of real estate on Highland Avenue. But not only size and scope capture attention: its verdant beauty, pressed hard against the commercial center that is downtown Hollywood and bounded by freeways that are at once the scourge and the saviour of Los Angeles, also serves to astonish and delight the observer. Since July 11, 1922, the official opening of "Symphonies Under the Stars," attended by some 5,000 people, millions have entered the area's leafy portals to be aroused, lulled, entranced, seduced, entertained, delighted by what arguably has been the widest-ranging array of outdoor performances and performers to be seen and heard anywhere.

Whatever the lure — symphony concerts, opera, operetta, ballet, theater, jazz, rock, folk, solo recitals, appearances by President Dwight D. Eisenhower or a President's daughter (Margaret Truman), celebrities from the concert, film, and dance worlds, Western Nights, Family Nights (Disney), children's concerts, special events such as Tribute to China, 1942, Salute to World Unity presented by Russian War Relief, 1943, Olympic Arts Festival concerts, 1984, World Cup Week concerts, 1994 — audiences have thronged and continue to throng to the Hollywood Bowl. As a landmark and an outdoor house of staged pleasure, the Bowl occupies a singular place in the affections of Southern Californians and people the world over.

From the very beginning, the Bowl audience was a unique one. Against various odds — frequently troublesome transportation, the climatic exigencies (it does often cool down considerably of a Los Angeles summer night, but it rarely rains!), delays at exit time, lines at the box office, lines at the restrooms (a problem at last, mercifully, almost extinct, as a result of the increased facilities built in the mid-1990s) — the audiences at the Bowl are notable for the kind of general goodwill and camaraderie that are, unfortunately, rarely experienced in the "outside" world. Far from the madding crowd, people from a variety of social strata find in the Bowl a refuge, a communal haven where tensions dissolve because society's artificial barriers seem to matter not at all. Friendly welcomes to strangers are common (people in neighboring boxes or benches rarely *remain* strangers at the Bowl); "please", "thank you", "may I borrow your bottle opener?", "certainly", and "after you", abound. In short, the atmos-

The tradition of a Bowl picnic takes a variety of forms.

Performers become audience members. Here conductor John Green with wife, Bonnie, and KFAC announcer Thomas Cassidy.

120

The Hollywood Bowl

phere resembles that of a favorite vacation spot: pleasure together is the watchword.

When "Symphonies Under the Stars" was born in 1922, the Bowl was to be the showcase for the Los Angeles Philharmonic. The public expected, and received, first-rate concert experiences. And they came to the Bowl with no little effort but with admirable equanimity. Those who were around in the early days tell of the many folk willing to arrive early in the afternoon so that they could spread blankets on the bench seats for family and friends. (Bench seats were unreserved until the 1950s.)

If hunger or thirst struck these loyal concertgoers, they had to leave their places to find a repast outside the amphitheater, for "Thou shalt not eat in the Bowl's seating area" was one of management's inflexible commandments. Until 1952, that is, when picnics in the boxes and bench areas were not only allowed, they were encouraged. After that noteworthy date, picnicking *in* the Bowl became and remains a very important part of the Bowl experience. Now, foods of every imaginable kind and wines of a plethora of labels are brought along by patrons or ordered from Fidler Enterprises, the Bowl's exclusive caterer, and consumed in box or bench. There are many well-developed official picnic areas located throughout the Bowl grounds outside the amphitheater proper. In recent years, unofficial picnic spots have appeared on walkways leading to the seating area. Here, on the asphalt, groups lay down a blanket and sit cross-legged, nonchalantly enjoying their pre-concert meal. One particularly unusual dining area was the one set up on the top of an RV, parked in the lot in back of the shell. Anything goes at the Bowl — virtually always with great good spirits.

For her first Bowl picnic outing, in 1952, Mrs. Norman Chandler had the classy (now gone) restaurant Perino's cater and serve her and her guests. In 1951, Dorothy Buffum Chandler, then a brand new member of the Bowl's Board of Directors and the wife of Norman Chandler, publisher of the *Los Angeles Times*, had spearheaded the historic "Save the Bowl" campaign. This succeeded in reopening the Bowl a short 12 days after it was forced to close because of a disastrous financial crunch caused by the egg laid at the box office by eight performances of *Die Fledermaus*.

Most Bowlgoers listen to a concert in various states of attention, appreciation, or euphoria. Unfortunately, some few think that the music is a good background for talking to their companions. One woman, Louise by name, waited patiently for her neighbors in the box in front of her to stop

their conversation. But exasperation finally took over, and she tapped the shoulder of one member of the gabbing duo and asked them both to please be quiet. The man responded with an ungentlemanly epithet; Louise's companion grasped the jacket of the offender, upbraiding him for his language. The talker, rising to his full height, accused the man of assault and said he was going to make a citizen's arrest. An usher was called, and the plaintiff and defendant, along with Louise, were taken to the manager's office. The case was rather quickly settled out of court, it should be reported. But the concert was ruined for all of them. Shhhh...

In the early days, word of the Hollywood Bowl and its wonders spread rapidly throughout the U.S. and even abroad. An article appearing in the *Dallas News* in 1930, datelined Los Angeles, July 26, is representative of the impression the amphitheater was making. Wrote Paul van Katwijk, "Anyone who entertains the slightest doubt of the musical inclinations of the American people should attend a concert at the Hollywood Bowl. He would come away with a new confidence in the future of music. Personally, I would risk the guess that of all the general interest in the higher forms of art, the one concerned with symphonic music is at the present time the most vital and intense." Heaping praise on the Bowl audience, he goes on to say, "Twenty thousand people do not go to the very decided trouble of parking 5,000 automobiles and climbing 150 feet to the top of an amphitheatre unless they are motivated by a very real interest. Night after night they fill this huge Hollywood Bowl to follow the programs with rapt attention. As much as 80 per cent of the music presented is serious, both classic and modern, and it follows that the masses of listeners must be genuinely interested in good music."

Considering its geographical location, the Hollywood Bowl has counted as part of its "purely American" audience many members of the film community. An account in the *Herald Express* (July 9, 1947) of the previous night's Bowl concert (Bruno Walter conducting, soprano Helen Traubel the soloist) reports the presence of such celebrities as Lana Turner with Tyrone Power and Jeanette MacDonald and her husband Gene Raymond (both couples pictured). Until 1942, the Bowl program books carried a listing of box holders, and the movie colony had considerable representation, e.g., Mr. and Mrs. Edward G. Robinson, Mrs. C. B. De Mille, Mr. and Mrs. Walt Disney, to name just a few. In more recent times, such luminaries as Rock Hudson, Danny Kaye, Louis Jourdan, Roddy McDowall, and Nancy Walker were frequent guests of the late Olive Behrendt, a longtime Philharmonic Association Board member, a dedicated worker for both the Philharmonic and the Bowl, and an inveterate Bowlgoer. Joseph Cotten was another Bowl habitué, as were the Kirk Douglases and box holder Steve McQueen. McQueen was adamant about having as much privacy as possible for himself and his family, and to that end he insisted that he be in the last row of boxes, out of the more publicity-prone glare of the lower Garden boxes. Testimonials for the Bowl from movie stars were not uncommon. There is a lovely picture of Claudette Colbert in the 1936 program book with a caption that reads, in part, [she] "rarely misses a symphony under the stars."

Film stars, directors, producers, and others from the "industry," political figures, corporate executives, musicians, artists, writers, and just plain folks, all are representative of the Hollywood Bowl audience. Indeed, the most striking aspect of the Bowl audience is its diversity. Even without taking an official poll, it is obvious to the eye that people of all ages and races and from all cultural, professional, and economic levels are attracted to the Bowl and *its* diversity. As long ago as 1925, Olin Downes, music critic of *The New York Times*, visited the Bowl and described the experience to his New York readers. In his report, he gave a bit of Bowl history, and then, in part, wrote, "It was Robert Haven Schauffler, if memory does not fail, who coined the phrase 'creative listening'. The meaning of the term comes home with particular force in the auditorium made by the mountains outside of Los Angeles and in the midst of an audience of over 30,000 [sic].... [The concerts] have a flavor different from any other concert known to me. The setting must be seen to be realized... it is no wonder that thousands upon thousands attend the four concerts given on as many evenings each week and that these people listen in a quiet and under a spell not known to audiences of concert halls, and that they learn, in their way, without lectures and guide books or analyses, to love and to worship music."

The attendance figure of 30,000 in the Olin Downes article was either the result of misprint or of misinformation. The capacity of Hollywood Bowl in 1925 was 15,000; it increased to 20,000 in 1926 and then, in 1952, due to specific changes in the seating, was reduced to just under 18,000, at which it now stands. One much-quoted attendance figure that exceeded the maximum at the time was the one registered on August 7, 1936; at that concert, some 26,410 people sat elbow-to-elbow, crowding the Bowl to hear the French coloratura soprano Lily Pons, a record that still stands and likely will never be broken, because of the fire safety regulations that came into effect

Celebrities are a frequent sight at the Bowl.
Top: Sidney Poitier.
Center: Kirk Douglas with Olive Behrendt.
Bottom: Johnny Carson and Harvey Korman.

Rain on the Bowl stage is a rare sight.

Danny Kaye cracks up the orchestra as well as the audience at one of his many Bowl appearances.

following her appearance. Before Pons, another notable attendance figure was for another songbird, this one Italian: Amelita Galli-Curci, who warbled for 21,873 people in June 1924.

In 1943, because of the war, attendance at the Bowl was limited to 5,000. When it was increased to 10,000 in 1944, Frank Sinatra drew the maximum. Continuing in the singers category, interest ran high for the appearance of Margaret Truman, the President's daughter, in August 1947: 11,100 came to be under-whelmed and to read in the *Los Angeles Times* the next day the sage comment of the music critic: "she needs more experience and a better music teacher." Apparently the President didn't threaten the L.A. writer as he did the D.C. critic (Paul Hume) who wrote ill of Harry's Margaret. Lest the impression be given that singers have been the biggest draw at the Bowl, mention must be made of at least three major instrumentalists of the past who packed them in: Jascha Heifetz, Artur Rubinstein, and Vladimir Horowitz. In the past two decades, however, a new star, neither of the vocal nor instrumental persuasion, has hit the box-office jackpot, namely, fireworks, the presence of which is virtually guaranteed to sell out the Bowl.

Since the 1970s, selling out the Bowl has been a frequent occurrence, which has helped to boost the attendance figure for each of the past several seasons to just under a million people. For many decades, Bowl volunteers have been responsible for bringing untold thousands to the outdoor concerts. The first volunteer group was the Patroness Committee, started in 1947 and still active. Carriage Clubs arranged special evenings for a limited number from as distant a locale as Riverside. The Area groups, which at one time were 26 in number (Burbank, Whittier, Long Beach, etc.) brought hundreds to at least one concert each season. Volunteers excited interest in the Bowl where none may have existed before. Through their dedication, they unquestionably created Bowl enthusi-asts who, after their initial indoctrination, became subscribers or at least Bowl regulars. Volunteers also had a very important hand in supporting Open House at the Bowl, the children's festival that has been convening for highly popular morning pro-grams and workshops six weeks each summer since 1969. The varied groups of volunteers, including

the more recently organized Friends of the Hollywood Bowl, are rightly credited with energizing Bowl attendance by bringing an ever more diverse audience to the concerts.

If it is tempting to characterize audiences as being either homogeneous or comprised of numbers of identifiable groups, it is still important to remember that every audience is made up of distinct individuals, with all the variety of personality and behavior that this implies. Stories about regular Bowlgoers abound, like the one about a woman who had the same box for years, and one summer called the office to complain about the draft that was bothering her. She thought it was caused by the removal of a tree near her seating location. Could it please be put back so that she could be comfortable again?

Many of the Bowl tales have to do with D & D — Death and Divorce. Take the zealots, for instance, who follow the obituaries and, recognizing the name of a box holder who has passed over, call the season ticket office immediately to stake a claim for the dearly departed's choice box. That action seldom works, however, for most box holders specify in their wills to whom the box is to go.

One divorce case in Bowl lore stands out among many. In this one, the husband was willing to waive ownership of the house so that he could take over their very desirable Bowl box. After the agreement was made and verified, the husband asked that the tickets not be mailed: he would send his secretary for them. In due time, the tickets were picked up and all seemed settled. But lo, on the first night of the season, when the husband arrived at the Bowl, he found the box occupied by — his wife! It was she who had picked up the tickets and was ready to exercise squatter's rights. Clearly, the husband was not about to stand still for that. The house manager had to assume the role of policeman, evict the wife (who, it is recalled, did not leave willingly), and hand the box over to its legal owner. Some people, it seems, will do almost anything to get their desired place at the Hollywood Bowl!

If one starts by saying that concertgoers are awed by the size and scope of the Bowl and by the whole Bowl ambience, one must end by saying that performers, too, experience a level of wonderment that is totally unique in the concert world. As wonderful as the magical expanse of seats, shell, stage, and hills may be when seen from the highest seats, the view from behind the footlights is breathtaking. Symphony musicians, conductors, instrumental or vocal soloists, jazz artists, recitalists, all respond with a real high to the powerful stimulus of realizing that there are thousands of expectant people out front. What a challenge: an unimaginably large audience to make music for, to communicate with, to reach, from the first row of boxes to the highest row of bench seats. This is what the Bowl is all about: fired-up performers and an audience ready for the taking. It takes two to tango.

What's a Performance Without an Audience?

BERNSTEIN TO BIG BIRD:

MUSIC EDUCATION AND YOUTH ACTIVITIES

BY JEANNETTE BOVARD

Leonard Bernstein, one of the most celebrated music educators of the 20th century, conducted at the Hollywood Bowl. But so, too, did Big Bird, Sesame Street resident and educator in his own right. This unlikely duo illustrates how the Hollywood Bowl reaches across age and educational barriers to share the joy of music.

Music education and fostering a love for the performing arts have been an integral part of the Hollywood Bowl's mission from the very beginning. Where else can one encounter such a vast and disparate audience for performances of the great classics? Who can even guess what percentage of each audience is musically educated, and to what degree? How many might be experiencing their very first live symphonic concert on any given night?

Beyond the concerts themselves, formal education programs have held an important place in Bowl history. Today, generations of children have enjoyed their first performing arts experiences during Open House at Hollywood Bowl, the perennially popular six-week multi-cultural arts festival inaugurated in 1969. But children were very much in the plans even during that very first season in 1922, when concerts especially for student audiences were presented to enhance the musical education offered in Southland classrooms. The Los Angeles Philharmonic Institute brought international renown to Southern California during its ten-year existence (1982-1991), becoming the West Coast's first major center specifically designed for orchestral training. School children, tourists, and nostalgia buffs alike have flocked to the Hollywood Bowl Museum since it opened in 1984, taking advantage of changing exhibits to inform or remind them of the Bowl's rich legacy and learn about specific aspects of music and musical performance.

Regular concert programming has always kept the relatively uninitiated in mind. "Family Nights" have been a staple of the annual schedule, as have concerts featuring the lighter side of the classical coin, fireworks, and other special effects enhancing the musical selections, and there are reduced ticket prices and similar incentives for students and large groups. Invitational rehearsals have given countless youngsters the opportunity to witness a symphony orchestra in action and gain an understanding of the process of preparation for performance.

Henry Mancini and Gregory
Lawrence Jefferson, 1991.

Educating the audiences of the future was a concern of the founding board in 1922, and is
arguably an even more important issue at the Bowl today.

"He who likes and demands good music in childhood is going to call for it throughout life,"
stated a concert review in the *Hollywood News* on August 1, 1923. "Musical taste, once formed, is not
likely to deteriorate. And for this reason, the children's concerts at the Hollywood Bowl have always
been first-class affairs.

"It was an inspiring sight, that audience of six thousand children which gathered at the Bowl,
July 18, to hear the program which Mr. Oberhoffer had arranged for them — a beautifully played
program, performed by the splendid orchestra to the keen delight of the youngsters...."

From the very first the Hollywood Bowl's summer concert seasons included concerts just for
children. "School concerts" took place on weekday afternoons and thousands of tickets were distributed to students free of charge through the public schools. "Extra tickets for children unprovided
through the school may be procured without cost at the Bowl Gate at the concert," stated the program
book.

During the inaugural season, 1922, special programs for children began at 5:00 p.m.
Children under 12, accompanied by parents or chaperones, were admitted free. These "Children's
Day" concerts included music by Bizet and Mendelssohn, Strauss waltzes, and "musical readings."
Special notices, such as the following, ran in the newspapers to find transportation for the less fortu-
nate among the young population: "If C.M. Pierce can get use of enough cars, every orphan in L.A.
will attend the Philharmonic concert at Hollywood Bowl Sunday afternoon." Indeed, according to
newspaper accounts, by the end of the season over 2,000 orphaned children had heard these concerts
— free of charge, of course.

Evening concerts were equally "student-friendly." Browsing through year after year of program books, one finds reference on an annual basis to student ticket opportunities and other special
offers, such as: "Children up to the age of 14 will be admitted to any Hollywood Bowl concert during

Pin awarded to outstanding young student musicians.

Celebrating graduation on Hat Day.

the 1934 season for 25 cents. This announcement is made by Symphony Society, Inc., in order to afford a greater number of children in Southern California an opportunity to hear Bowl concerts and see Bowl ballets. This price will prevail on solo and novelty nights as well as on Tuesday and Saturday nights." Opportunities such as these were maintained even during the World War II years when the Bowl was limited to a quarter of its capacity due to the "emergency."

Older "young audiences" were equally courted. An article in the Hollywood Bowl program of 1937 remarked on the large number of college-aged audience members taking advantage of student tickets. "Parents will tell you that there is no reason why youngsters between the ages of 16 and 21 should trade an evening of dancing and dining for the Hollywood Bowl — no reason but one: they enjoy it!"

Gainful — and tuneful — employment was also a draw for the teen-to-twenty crowd. The Bowl's ushering crew has traditionally been staffed by students, many pursuing music studies and finding the summer job both enjoyable and a valuable learning experience. So popular was the job — in spite of the fact that ushers were essentially unpaid volunteers during the first half-century of Bowl history — that on many evenings far more attendants were on duty than were needed. George London is possibly the most famous of the Bowl's former ushers, but an untold number of musicians and music lovers have listed and will continue to list the summertime experience on their resumés.

A strong link has always existed between music education in the schools and the Philharmonic's summer and winter concerts. "The music program in our public schools is aided immeasurably by the variety and quality of the musical activities that are carried on in metropolitan Los Angeles," noted the Hollywood Bowl program in 1950, citing the L.A. Philharmonic's winter series of Symphonies For Youth, opera performances, chamber music concerts, "and through the generosity of the Hollywood Bowl Association a large number of our students are privileged to attend the Symphonies Under the Stars who otherwise would be unable to do so."

Violinist Ivry Gitlis instructs a
young student.

"Mr. Oberhoffer's program was made up of numbers of moderate comprehensiveness, not the deepest, of course, but not a note of trashy or undignified music." (*Hollywood News*, 8/1/23)

Accessibility and quality have been two overriding characteristics of children's concert programming. Conductor and pianist Ernest Schelling ("Uncle Ernest" to his many fans, conductor at the time of the New York Philharmonic's Young People's Concerts, and himself a former child prodigy) set the pace for family concerts to come. His program on July 20, 1935 listed Purcell's Trumpet Prelude, Schubert's *Marche Militaire*, excerpts from Bizet's *L'Arlésienne* Suite No. 2, Dukas' *The Sorcerer's Apprentice*, MacDowell's *Woodland Sketches*, his own *Suite Fantastique*, Tchaikovsky's *Nutcracker Suite*, and Weber's *Freischütz* Overture, with Wagner's *Ride of the Valkyries* the rousing finale. Uncle Ernest illustrated his program with "colorful Lantern Slides...which he has gathered on his travels to the four corners of the earth." The lantern slides have given way to more sophisticated visuals, but Uncle Ernest's musical selections have stood the test of time and are as likely to crop up on a program in 1996 as they did throughout the decades.

Child-pleasing Disney tunes have been a staple of "Family Night" programs since the 1950s. But so, too, have Beethoven, Brahms, Tchaikovsky, Gershwin, and the greats of the American musical theater. Similarly, the roster of guest artists has been varied and impressive, featuring many of the most popular entertainers of the day. Stokowski himself directed some of the earliest programs. Lionel

Barrymore narrated the world premiere of his own composition, *Hallowe'en*, A Fantasy for Orchestra and Voices, for the family audience of 1945. Isaac Stern played the Beethoven Violin Concerto for the College Night audience in 1953. Danny Kaye delighted Bowl audiences of all ages on several occasions; in 1957 he shared the bill with soprano Dorothy Kirsten, pianist Leonard Pennario, and Lola Montes and her Spanish Dancers. Meredith Willson presided in an elaborately-staged "Evening with the 'Music Man' " in 1960. And who wouldn't love to have been in the audience on July 20, 1946 for the "Family Night" tribute to Jerome Kern, conducted by Johnny Green, that starred Judy Garland, Kathryn Grayson, Lena Horne, Tony Martin, Virginia O'Brien, Bill Roberts, Frank Sinatra, and Robert Walker!

The most popular and wide-ranging of all the Hollywood Bowl's programs for children was born in 1969, the brainchild of the Bowl's then-newly-appointed general manager Ernest Fleischmann, aided by volunteer leader Helen Wolford.

Mrs. Wolford had been active in children's theater projects at the University of California, Los Angeles (UCLA) before being asked to work on children's programming for the Hollywood Bowl Volunteers. Her first event, in 1963, seemed doomed to failure, as she recalls. "It was a concert at 10:00 a.m. at the Bowl. We printed 5,000 tickets, but fully expected nobody to show up." Much to everyone's surprise, 10,000 eager young audience members and their parents filled the Bowl.

"It became obvious that these types of programs were needed," she notes. "Then, when Ernest Fleischmann came with his strong support for this type of programming, things got bigger and better than ever before with Open House at Hollywood Bowl."

That first year advertised "daytime entertainment for everyone from 6 to 66" and featured theater, puppets, magic, music, mime, and dance every hour and half-hour from 10:00 a.m. to 12:30 p.m. Performances took place on the Box Office Plaza with Ebony Showcase and Ling Lee, "the famed Chinese musician," the inaugural acts in what has become an endless string of child-pleasing entertainments. The San Fernando Valley State College Youth Theater, CalState Long Beach Youth Theater, and the Santa Barbara High School Mime Troupe (Les Masques Blancs) joined Benjy's Puppet Pals on the Open House roster in 1969, beginning a tradition of showcasing both ethnically and artistically diverse, as well as younger, performers — a sure-fire way of sparking a young audience's interest and encouraging other budding performers.

Daniel Lewis was co-artistic director of the Los Angeles Philharmonic Institute in 1982.

André Previn, conducting the Institute Orchestra in 1987.

Through the years this performing arts festival for children has become a must-do summer-time activity for Southern California youngsters and a prototype for similar programs throughout the nation. Years before diverse programming became a staple of arts organizations country-wide, Open House defined a goal of cultural enrichment that would open the entire world, not just a small slice of it, to its audiences.

Some of the most popular acts that have played the Open House stage over more than two-and-a-half decades have been the Ballet Folklórico-Mexicana de Graciela Tapia, Bob Baker Marionette Theatre, East-West Players, Sonny Criss' Jazz Quartet, R'Wanda Lewis Afro-American Dance Company, Opera À La Carte, Aman Folk Ensemble, Rob Bowers (Open House's first Master of Ceremonies), Odessa Balalaikas, Teatro de los Puppets, the Mark Taper Forum's Improvisational Theatre Project, Fujima Kansuma Kai, Korean Classical Music and Dance Company, Plaza de la Raza Players, Viji Prakash, Chief Red Dawn and Blue Eagle, Dan Crow, the South Bay Ballet, Lula and Afro Brazil, San Andreas Brass, and We Tell Stories, among many others.

Providing continuity, familiarity, and child-pleasing interactive performance have been the husband and wife team of John and Pam Wood — better known as J. P. Nightingale — emcees on the Open House stage since 1974.

More than just performances, Open House has included hands-on arts experiences since its second season. Kay Clapp, a Bowl volunteer and mother of two of that year's youngest audience members, suggested the interactive component. "Joan Boyett [who began producing Open House in 1970 and, subsequently, other Los Angeles Philharmonic/Hollywood Bowl educational programs] invited conversations about what the audience would like," remembers Clapp. "So we mentioned that it would be terrific to have a project that was hands-on." Thus began the workshops following each Open House performance that give young audiences opportunities to participate in activities related to the day's presentations. Divided into age-appropriate work groups, youngsters learn to sing, dance, make an instrument, or work on ethnic crafts related to what they have just seen on the Open House stage.

Right from the beginning, Ernest Fleischmann insisted that the Open House experience should also include a visit by the children to the Bowl's huge amphitheater in order to observe part of the rehearsal by the Philharmonic and, of course, to take part in another Bowl tradition, a picnic.

Approximately 36,000 children attend Open House at Hollywood Bowl each year. Today, parents who first enjoyed the performances as children are bringing their own offspring to share the enjoyment of one of the longest-running hits in Bowl history. Not surprisingly, some of today's professional artists credit the Bowl program with inspiring their creativity and interest in the field.

Career-building, in fact, was the major component of one Hollywood Bowl program. The Los Angeles Philharmonic Institute (LAPI) focused on the future of the musical arts from the standpoint of the performers rather than the audience. And the measure of its success — in spite of the financial strain that led to suspension of the program in December 1991 after a decade of increasing renown — can be seen on the rosters of orchestras worldwide. LAPI alumni hold posts with major orchestras literally from coast-to-coast and abroad. Of the 757 instrumentalists who had participated in the program from its inception until the tenth, and final, year, 257 were employed as orchestral musicians as of summer 1991. This number included two members of the Los Angeles Philharmonic — principal percussionist Raynor Carroll and violinist Mitchell Newman — and the Hollywood Bowl Orchestra's principal horn, John Reynolds.

Unique to the Institute was its focus on young conductors in addition to instrumentalists. "Conducting Fellows," chosen by audition, as were the musicians, were given the opportunity to rehearse and perform a wide repertory with the Institute Orchestra. In the ever-changing world of musical ensembles, the names of LAPI alumni will continue to appear on orchestra rosters and concert programs for decades. Among those who have captured major posts are two who participated in the inaugural session — Jahja Ling, resident conductor of the Cleveland Orchestra as well as music director of the Florida Orchestra; and Eiji Oue, music director of the Minnesota Orchestra. More recently, Keith Lockhart, LAPI Fellow in 1989, was named conductor of the Boston Pops Orchestra. David Alan Miller, an alumnus of the 1985 and 1986 summer Institutes, subsequently became associate conductor of the Los Angeles Philharmonic and associate director of the Institute before accepting the post of music director of the Albany Symphony.

"The Los Angeles Philharmonic Institute evolved as the result of discussions about the future of the American symphony orchestra between the late Leonard Bernstein and Ernest Fleischmann, executive vice president and managing director of the Los Angeles Philharmonic. They agreed that there was a profound need for a concentrated, focused program at the highest professional level to prepare gifted young instrumentalists and conductors for orchestral careers," stated a brochure describing the genesis of this far-reaching program.

The inaugural season of the West Coast's first major orchestral training center included all the elements that were to characterize the Institute experience:

· A roster of enthusiastic and gifted young musicians and conductors from diverse backgrounds and geographic regions.

· A faculty comprised of internationally distinguished conductors and instrumentalists, including members of the Los Angeles Philharmonic and artists scheduled to appear during the summer at the Bowl. The legendary Bernstein and Daniel Lewis, the reigning dean of Southern California conducting teachers, served as artistic directors that first summer, with flutist Jean-Pierre Rampal and conductors Christopher Hogwood and Michael Tilson Thomas also on the faculty.

Open House workshop activities.

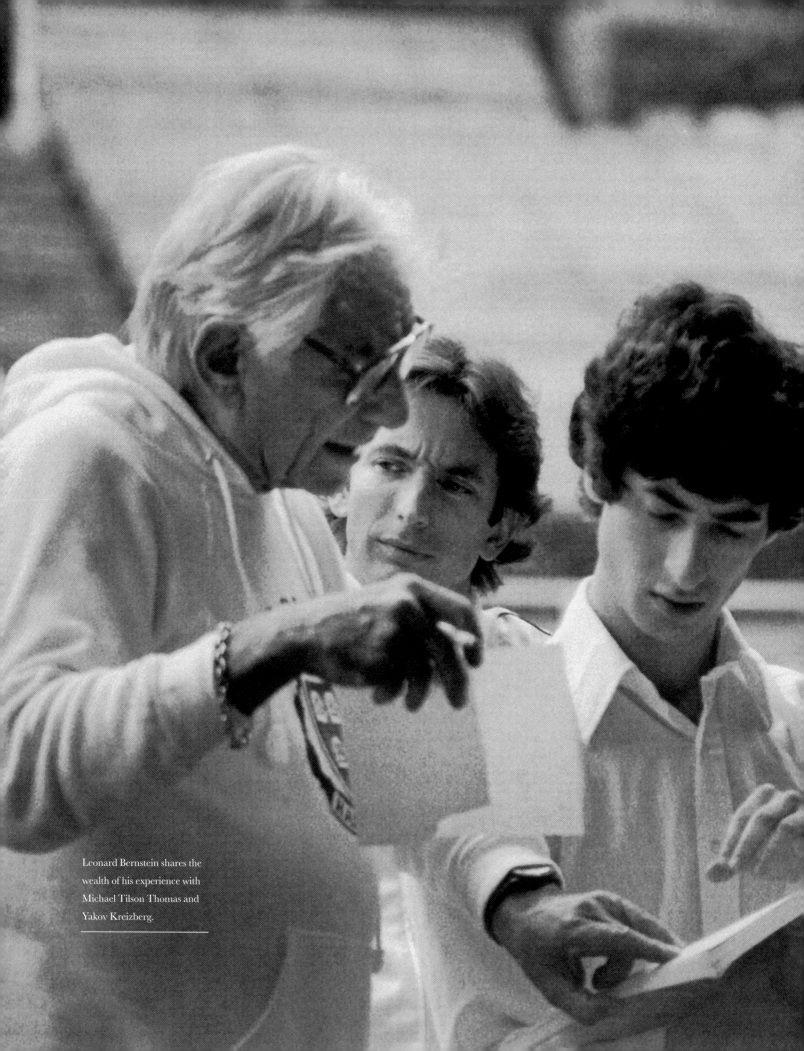

Leonard Bernstein shares the
wealth of his experience with
Michael Tilson Thomas and
Yakov Kreizberg.

· A challenging curriculum, with rehearsals, workshops, and master classes designed to work on different aspects of orchestral performance.

· The unmatched experience of rehearsing for and performing in a series of orchestral concerts at the Hollywood Bowl under the batons of major conductors, including a joint concert with the Los Angeles Philharmonic, plus orchestral and chamber music concerts in other local venues.

· A collegiate home base, UCLA, where the students lived together, practiced together, and socialized together, in comfortable and attractive surroundings. The Institute moved its base of operation to Cal State Northridge for the 1984 season, when UCLA housed athletes participating in the Olympic Games.

The rosters of students and faculty changed from summer to summer, but the spirit remained as bright as ever, as evidenced in consistently glowing concert reviews throughout the decade.

Leonard Bernstein with Institute student Michael Barrett, 1983.

"The young players of the institute rose to the musical occasion and accomplished the recognizable modernist style effortlessly [in an all-Lutoslawski program conducted by the venerable composer himself]. Not all American orchestras have this kind of versatility. Or immaculate instrumental skills." (*Los Angeles Times*, August 11, 1989)

The distinguished musicians who guided the Institute as artistic directors included, in addition to Bernstein and Lewis (1982), Michael Tilson Thomas (1983-85), Sir Charles Groves (1986), Lukas Foss and André Previn (1987), and Lynn Harrell (1988-91). Among those who shared their expertise as members of the faculty were John Adams, Josef Gingold, Erich Leinsdorf, Witold Lutoslawski, Simon Rattle, Esa-Pekka Salonen, Leonard Slatkin, Yuri Temirkanov, David Zinman, Emanuel Ax, Yefim Bronfman, Cho-Liang Lin, Nadia Salerno-Sonnenberg, the Bartók Quartet, and the Emerson Quartet, to name just a few.

Berlioz' *Le Corsaire* Overture brought the curtain up on the Institute's inaugural Hollywood Bowl concert on July 25, 1982 with Conducting Fellow Eiji Oue holding the distinction of being the first to publicly conduct the Institute Orchestra at the Bowl. Daniel Lewis presided over Prokofiev's Fifth Symphony, while the podium spotlight shone on another Conducting Fellow, Leonid Grin, in Mendelssohn's Violin Concerto, with Julie Rosenfeld, the Institute Orchestra's concertmaster, as soloist.

The varied study and performance repertory each year was chosen to cover a broad range of orchestral experience, from concert hall favorites (Bach, Beethoven, Brahms, Mozart, Schubert, Strauss, Tchaikovsky) to 20th-century masters (Bartók, Copland, Stravinsky, Varèse). Memorable were the concert performances of Puccini's *La bohème* in 1985 and Beethoven's *Fidelio* in 1986.

New-music concerts provided opportunities for exploration into the sound worlds of Cage, Messiaen, Reich, and Takemitsu; the challenge and excitement of presenting world premieres; the stimulation of working with composers such as John Adams, John Harbison, and Lutoslawski. The 1991 (final) season included the world premiere of the first work commissioned specifically for the Los Angeles Philharmonic Institute (Edward Knight's *Granite Island*), a project conceived to add yet another dimension to the Institute's performing agenda.

There was also a major chamber music component to the Institute's activities, with repertoire preparation supervised by some of the leading exponents of this more intimate art form. Institute chamber ensembles regularly performed at such venues as UCLA's Schoenberg Hall, the John Anson Ford Amphitheatre, and the University of Judaism's Gindi Auditorium, home of the Los Angeles Philharmonic Chamber Music Society.

A highlight of each season for students and audiences alike was the Institute Orchestra's joint concert with the Los Angeles Philharmonic, an opportunity for the younger musicians to perform side by side with their Philharmonic counterparts. Leonard Bernstein was on the podium for this extravaganza in the inaugural season, with the massed forces performing the Adagietto from Mahler's Fifth Symphony and Tchaikovsky's *Francesca da Rimini*. Berlioz' *Symphonie fantastique*, Beethoven's Ninth Symphony, Mahler's Symphony No. 1 and Symphony No. 8 (Symphony of a Thousand), Rachmaninoff's Second Symphony, and Sibelius' *Finlandia* and Symphony No. 2 were just some of the works performed by the joint orchestras in subsequent years. In 1987, "Mr. Hollywood Bowl Marathon" himself, the indefatigable Lukas Foss, revived the Marathon Concert which had become a popular Hollywood Bowl attraction in the early 1970s, giving the two orchestras plenty to do, both together and apart! The marathon was brought back again in the Bowl's 75th Anniversary Season, as Lukas Foss returned to conduct the Los Angeles Philharmonic and the Los Angeles Chamber Orchestra in a "Best of the Marathons" evening.

Although tour groups, Open House patrons, and interested music-lovers have always been welcome to observe rehearsals at the Hollywood Bowl, the most formal of the rehearsal-based programs was initiated in 1991. Members of the Los Angeles Philharmonic's Community Advisory Committee saw the Bowl debut of 14-year-old flutist Gregory Lawrence Jefferson as an opportunity for students to meet an inspiring young musician and role model. One hundred youngsters from Los Angeles-area schools, including the Los Angeles County High School for the Arts, the Los Angeles Music and Art School, the Colburn School of Performing Arts, the Compton YWCA and 24th Street

School were invited to attend the morning rehearsal and then to meet the young flutist and members of the Los Angeles Philharmonic during a picnic lunch at the Bowl.

Based on the success of this event, the Student Rehearsal Program was created, with the goal of matching groups with artists who could serve as role models. One particularly inspiring session took place with Evelyn Glennie, the internationally renowned percussionist who is severely hearing-impaired, and groups of youngsters also challenged by hearing difficulties. Over the past decade, approximately 3,000 students have participated in these invitational rehearsals, which also include a tour of the Hollywood Bowl Museum as an integral part of the day.

The Hollywood Bowl Museum, another relatively recent project in the Bowl's history, opened its doors on June 29, 1984, through a partnership between the County of Los Angeles and the Los Angeles Philharmonic Association. In 1995, the Museum was rededicated and renamed the Edmund D. Edelman Hollywood Bowl Museum in honor of the former Los Angeles County Supervisor who was its key supporter.

With 3,000 square feet of museum space on two floors, the renovated Hollywood Bowl Museum includes a permanent display on the history of the Hollywood Bowl; a gallery for temporary exhibitions on musical and related topics; and video, audio, and interactive computer facilities. Admission is free and the facility is open year-round.

The changing exhibits have highlighted various aspects of the Hollywood Bowl's rich artistic legacy as well as more general musical topics. The opening exhibit in 1984 focused, appropriately, on the rich legacy of the Bowl itself with "The Hollywood Bowl: A Vision for Music." A retrospective of recorded sound, "Sound Waves," was installed in 1986. "A Bowl for All Nations" in 1988 displayed non-Western musical instruments, and ethnomusicology was the topic of "Rhythms and Roots: Five Musical Families" in 1989. The highly acclaimed exhibit on European emigré artists of the 1930s, "Exiles in Paradise," was created at the Bowl Museum in 1991 and later displayed in Germany, Austria, and Switzerland. "New Sounds in New Shapes" in 1992 gave Museum guests the opportunity not only to see, but also to hear, innovative and unusual contemporary music instruments. "Music in Films: The Sound Behind the Image," 1993, was a particularly appropriate exhibit for the Hollywood-based facility, and the following year the Museum celebrated the Los Angeles Philharmonic's 75th Anniversary Season with "Music for a Great City." A variety of smaller exhibits has been incorporated into the Museum space simultaneously with the major displays.

The Bowl Museum's educational program combines cultural history and music education with changing components based on current exhibitions. Tours are free and activities include a walking tour of the Hollywood Bowl, an exploration of Museum exhibitions, videos, and hands-on participation.

Lectures, panels, and concerts have been an important facet of Museum operations since its inception, adding variety and diversity to the programming at the Bowl.

As the Edmund D. Edelman Hollywood Bowl Museum begins its second decade, its director, Carol Merrill-Mirsky, looks forward to new, innovative, and expanding programs, mindful of the need to nourish, educate, and attract the audiences of the future. With the diminishing availability of music education in our schools, institutions such as the Hollywood Bowl and the Los Angeles Philharmonic are continually striving to fill the gaps and encourage both youngsters and their parents to explore the exciting, stimulating world of classical music. This is where the Hollywood Bowl plays a significant role in our society: ever-appealing and always eager to educate, and to share musical pleasure with one and all.

Big Bird leads as Assistant Conductor Sidney Harth looks on.

GROWING UP AT THE HOLLYWOOD BOWL

BY STEPHANIE FLEISCHMANN

Some people grow up in one house, with a single set of hidden stairs leading to an attic that's still there, even after its fledgling inhabitants have grown and gone. Piles of childhood scribbles, heaps of tiny trucks, paper bags full of dolls' clothes and unplayed instruments, dented cornets, cracked oboes, and dusty recorders, sit packed away in boxes, waiting to be sifted through and mulled over, waiting for the next generation, when they'll be used again. As I've grown, the houses have changed. There has been no single attic, but there has always been one constant: summers at the Hollywood Bowl.

I grew up at the Hollywood Bowl, to the tune of a thousand steps, as good as any attic stairs I've climbed in any one of the several houses I lived in as a child. Those attics are all off-limits now, from revisitation and remembering; they belong to other, unknown families. But the concrete steps at the Bowl are still there, waiting to be climbed every time I go back. Ascending these steps to sections X, Y, and Z, the Bowl's open-air *paradiso*, the memories are in the body. They are in the sounds and the smells and the sights that do not change, even as the columns which edge the stage transform into champagne-bubble balls bouncing against the ceiling of the shell, even as acoustics are tweaked via the mysteries of a science that is at once as old as the ancient amphitheater of Epidaurus and as new as Suntory Hall.

Climb the thousand steps (can it really be only 168!?!) to reach the top, where the air is thin and the camaraderie of the listeners who have paid less than the price of a movie to hear a Mozart symphony or *The Rite of Spring* is tangible, and you will see that the musicians are no bigger than ants and you will hear how their music rising toward the heavens sounds as crystalline and alive as it does from the swanky boxes way down below. The years pass, and this summer people will no doubt bring along portable cellular phones with their picnics, but these other things don't change: the night smells of sunbaked hillside, the sweet rock dust and evergreen and eucalyptus; the faint wheeze of smog at the base of your throat after you have made the climb. These are reassuring, familiar sensations.

This year the Hollywood Bowl celebrates its 75th birthday. Last Fourth of July, from a roof in Williamsburg, Brooklyn, I watched the Macy's fireworks display exploding in glorious style over the

John Mauceri and the Hollywood Bowl Orchestra with the USC Trojan Marching Band and fireworks.

East River against the sky-scraping contours of the Chrysler Building and its surround, and silently toasted my own 25th anniversary with the Hollywood Bowl. Three thousand miles away, the Bowl's annual Fourth of July fireworks concert was about to begin with a roll of the snare drum. Nobody needed to tell me this; I knew it in my blood as surely as I know that the moon rises and sets. For whether I am there in body or merely via power of mind, the Bowl is for me one of the few sure things in life.

The Hollywood Bowl is Hollywood old and new; it is the living, breathing past and present (and future) encompassed within a single hollow in the earth. It is a geological phenomenon that has survived the fickle swells of fame and fortune in that quick-blinking, fashion-conscious land of so-called mindless entertainment, the birthplace of the silver screen. A cultural force that has endured the throes of erosion and a capricious, lurching earth, it continues to endure a dismal recession and the current political climate, which is so hostile to the arts, it threatens their very survival. But above all, the Hollywood Bowl is a container for my own private history. It is the map by which I've learned to read my father, the Bowl's mastermind for more than a quarter of a century — a man who I used to believe could change the flight path of an airplane with a single, whispered bark into the telephone in his box. When I was little I knew him as a shaper of sound. In those days he seemed to hone music as if it were sculpture with his finely tuned chisel of an ear, night after summer night issuing instructions over his hotline phone. I remember him stalking rehearsals on hot summer mornings.

I was hardly eight years old, but I remember how the musicians would work, refining a phrase — and how he listened. Sometimes the conductor would even turn around and ask about the balance. My father would, of course, always have a ready answer. It was there, at the Hollywood Bowl, that I first began to understand the sweat and gristle that goes into making great music, and by association, other forms of art. It was what I would call an initiation. Ever since then, the Bowl has been a place of rite of passage for me, a place of firsts.

My first summer job was at the Bowl. I was fourteen. I applied for the position of usher, filled out the requisite form, interviewed sitting on a cold metal chair somewhere deep in the maze of concrete passageways beneath the stage, and was almost stunned that I passed muster. I would earn minimum wage, $3-something an hour. The only hitch: "The Big E sent her," read a mysterious note on my application. The Big E. My father. He would not live this one down. As the first-born child of The Big E, I didn't have to work my way up to the front like most people did; I was stationed on the first prom my very first summer, just below my father's control center of a box. Sitting in on the ushers meetings, however, in the empty house during those brief moments when the Bowl was ours alone before the audience was allowed to filter in, I only half-listened while head usher Raoul Pinno, our mustachioed leader, delivered his daily strategic briefing in a tone as suave as it was disciplinary.

Half-listened, because I was busy indulging in that most Spartan of daydreams: anonymity. Imagining that I was just like all the other ushers — that I was not the boss's daughter — I would breathe a fleeting sigh of relief. Certainly there was some secret part of me that liked the faintly glamorous tinge of infamy my station in life at the Bowl carried with it. But the greater part of me yearned to remain a peon. There was an odd thrill, I realized, in playing the very tiniest part in the workings of a great, enormous institution, one that put on concerts under the stars night after night, often for almost 18,000 listeners, in a fashion that seemed to me as seamless and breathtaking as the velveteen oval of night sky hanging above us, with its streamlined slash of searchlights criss-crossing the heavens, announcing: Here sit together thousands upon thousands of people, of all colors and shapes and sizes and places of birth, musicians and listeners alike, all partaking in a singular, unifying experience, that of the chasm-bridging, soul-transporting power of music.

Before concerts, and during intermissions, I zipped up and down my set of stairs, showing patrons to their seats, or I stood at my post, nearly swimming amid the endless river of faces that streamed by. To pass the time, I practiced the awkward art of throwing smiles in the direction of my favorite roving ushers and red-jacketed program boys. I began to revel in my power to draw others to me when fixed in one place. I became skilled at it. I got myself asked out on my first date. By a program boy no less, who drove a pickup truck; it was a disaster of the most mismatched kind.

Sitting (at last, sitting!) on the concrete steps after the long hours of pre-concert standing, huddling in the shadows thrown by the elevated boxes, and listening to the music low to the ground, where you could be closer to your thoughts, I would lean back and stretch my neck to the sky and drink in the stars. This was even better than being an audience member. The audience sat on hard wooden benches that were known to plant splinters into aching bottoms; or in green metal-and-canvas director's chairs that scraped whenever anybody moved and, exposed as they were to the elements, occasionally wore straight through with a thundering rip when someone sat down too quickly with too much girth.

After intermission, when the world was safely settled in its seats and I had had my fill of listening for the night, I would punch out before the concert was over and hang out in the parking lot just beyond the backstage entrance with my new usher friends, who were mostly older than I and from parts of the city I'd never ever been to but would soon visit. I would glory in the semi-forbidden quality of our whispering and gossiping that fermented in the dark, to the strains of music coming from the other side of the shell, where, on the brilliantly lit stage, world-class performances were taking place before thousands of silent, rapt listeners.

Those first couple of years, before I was old enough to drive, we took the bus to work — four buses, actually. I rode across town with my sister, who was an usher too, and my brother and his bevy of friends, who were part of the small army of white-jumpsuited garbage boys called "runners" that moved through the Bowl before concerts like a pack of wolves, rangy and lean and sunburned, collecting the remains of picnic dinners, cracking jokes as they sidled by. The bus ride was an epic journey, and we had to set out early to get to work on time. At around 4:30 on those hot summer afternoons, the slow-moving chariot was flooded with a golden, smog-flecked light that made you feel as if you were inside a moving picture. The wash of changing terrain seen from up high on that series of crosstown buses gave me my first grasp of the geography of L.A. beyond the overprotected, ultra-segregated fold of Brentwood and the West side where I'd grown up. We would get off at the

Peppertree Lane.

Growing Up at the Hollywood Bowl

illustrious corner of Hollywood and Vine. Walking up Highland from Hollywood Boulevard I made my first acquaintance with an older L.A., with a history that perhaps harkened back to before the ranch houses, to a time when the city was something more than a necklace of mini-malls strung out in all directions.

The Hollywood Bowl is of that time. Visit it during the day, when all is quiet, and you will feel how its surrounding hills seem to reverberate with the sound waves of great performances of summers past, summers spanning three-quarters of a century, the notes of a Koussevitzky or a Piatigorsky or a Bernstein or a Lily Pons still somehow hanging in the air, making themselves felt. I have sometimes wondered whether, perhaps because the place is still functioning as it was originally intended to, it hasn't become one of those points where time folds in on itself, where eras and dimensions and planes rub up against each other, just barely overlapping, like those supposed places of convergence that register invisible force-fields of energy under the eye of an ultraviolet camera.

Perhaps it is merely because I have always known I could come back to it, because of those 25 years of shared history, that the Bowl holds such resonance for me. Or, more likely, it's because when I was very small, it was there that I got to be Queen of the Hill. Picture this: A small kingdom where your father is king and you are the princess; you can go anywhere, through any gate or barricade — all you have to do is stomp about and white-jacketed ushers undo ropes and wave you through. The stars shine down upon you and the lasers blaze across the skies, proclaiming that you are here. You are here, and just to make sure nobody has forgotten, you will trot backstage at intermission, careful not to spill your Styrofoam cup of hot chocolate, and say hello to Mr. Mehta; then you will peek out through the stage door at the thousands of people, visitors for a night to your kingdom, chatting and strolling, waiting, enthralled, for the second half to begin, and you will watch approvingly from your place of honor as the stagehands, who are always ready with a wink and a ruffle of your head, haul grand pianos and harps across the stage. And when you have had enough of all that, you will trot back to your box and wrap yourself in a blanket against the cold night air, and you will tilt your head back and close your eyes, and with the stars and the music swirling inside your brain, you will dream.

Editors' note

For nearly 50 years the Hollywood Bowl Patroness Committee has devoted considerable time and effort to enhancing awareness of the Hollywood Bowl and generating funds to support it.

They generously underwrote this comprehensive history of the Bowl so that proceeds could provide for the ongoing maintenance of the artists' rooms, which were recently renovated as a result of the Committee's efforts.

Putting long hours into the preparation of this book on behalf of the Committee were Bee Jay Di Vall, Barbara Harris, Jeanne Johnson, and Louise Jones. Their contribution to all aspects of the project was invaluable.

Over the years, the Patroness Committee has honored artists and others who have contributed to the success of the Hollywood Bowl. The honorees have included:

Humphrey Burton
Mrs. Norman Chandler
Mary Costa
Richard Crooks
Christian Dior
Ernest Fleischmann
Lukas Foss
David Frisina
Jakob Gimpel
Mona Golabek
John Green
Sir Charles Groves
Lynn Harrell
Jascha Heifetz
Bronislaw Kaper
Dorothy Kirsten
Daniel Lewis
Henry Mancini
John Mauceri
Leonard Pennario
Gregor Piatigorsky
Anita Priest
John Raitt
Kurt Reher
Paul Salamunovich
Michael Tilson Thomas
Barry Tuckwell
Roger Wagner
Elinor Remick Warren
Sidney Weiss
John Williams
Meredith Willson

"Late Comers," an original
wood block by Franz Geritz

CONTRIBUTORS

Editor *MICHAEL BUCKLAND* was born in England and educated in New Zealand; he has worked internationally as a writer, creative director and marketing executive. Previously working with The Philadelphia Orchestra, he currently serves as Director of Marketing and Communications for the Los Angeles Philharmonic Association.

Musicologist and critic *JOHN HENKEN* holds a Ph.D. from UCLA in historical musicology. A former staff writer for the *Los Angeles Times* and former director of publications for the Los Angeles Philharmonic, he is widely published in both academic and popular periodicals.

CAROL McMICHAEL REESE is a writer, curator, and independent scholar, her work focusing on 19th- and 20th-century urbanism. Trained as an art historian, she teaches at the Southern California Institute of Architecture.

Professor and Chair of the Dance Program at the American University in Washington DC, *NAIMA PREVOTS* has authored numerous articles on dance. She is currently finishing books about art and public policy and choreographer Erick Hawkins. Other books include *Dancing in the Sun, Hollywood Choreographers 1915-1937*, and *American Pageantry, A Movement for Art and Democracy*.

HERBERT GLASS' writings on music appear in the *Los Angeles Times*, *Gramophone*, and *The Strad*. He is also a contributor to the *New Grove Dictionary of Music and Musicians*.

LISA MITCHELL is an actor and writer whose articles on the media appear in various publications, including the *Los Angeles Times* and *The Directors Guild of America News*. She is working on a book about Cecil B. De Mille and the making of "The Ten Commandments."

Writer and lyricist *GENE LEES* has been editor of *Down Beat* and a contributing editor and columnist for *Stereo Review*, *High Fidelity*, and *American Film*. He is the publisher of *The Jazzletter* and a lyricist, noted particularly for his English-language versions of songs by Antonio Carlos Jobim.

GEORGE VARGA is the pop music critic for the *San Diego Union Tribune* and Copley News Service. His work has also appeared in *Jazz Times*, *Spin*, and other publications, and he has written liner notes for six albums including Michael Brecker's Grammy-winning release "Don't Try This at Home." His first Hollywood Bowl concert was the inaugural Playboy Jazz Festival in 1979; he has been back many times since.

DENNIS BADE is director of publications for the Los Angeles Philharmonic. Previously he was editorial director for the American division of the French record label, Harmonia Mundi, and served as programming coordinator and executive producer of records programming for public radio station KUSC.

ORRIN HOWARD, who annotated Los Angeles Philharmonic programs for more than 20 years while serving the Orchestra as director of publications and archives, is currently the Philharmonic's archives advisor.

JEANNETTE BOVARD, former associate director of publications and archives for the Los Angeles Philharmonic Association, currently holds the post of director of development for Friends Outside in Los Angeles County. She has also served as a publicity and editorial consultant for the Pasadena Symphony and has worked with numerous other arts organizations on the development of instructional materials.

STEPHANIE FLEISCHMANN recently completed her first novel, *Night Baby*, for which she was awarded a New York Foundation For The Arts Fellowship. Her plays have been developed at New York's Public Theater and performed Off-Off Broadway, as well as in the L.A. Theatre Works radio theater series on KCRW. She has been a Fellow at the McDowell Colony and at Hedgebrook.

ACKNOWLEDGMENTS

Any project as complex as the history of such an institution as the Hollywood Bowl requires the cooperation and support of many people. Here are the names of those who have not already been thanked elsewhere in this book:

Alice Asquith and Christi Brockway, Hollywood Bowl
John F. Beringhele, International Alliance of Theatrical Stage Employees, Local 33
Lance Bowling, Cambria Archives
Gretchen Citrin, Los Angeles Philharmonic
Robert Cushman, Academy of Motion Picture Arts and Sciences
Bill Farley, Playboy Enterprises, Inc.
Julio Gonzalez, Music Center Archives
Ann Gray, Balcony Press
Steve LaCoste, Los Angeles Philharmonic Archives
Emily Laskin, Los Angeles Philharmonic
Carol Merrill-Mirsky, Hollywood Bowl Museum
Donn Weller, for the delightful drawings you see throughout this book

Finally, special thanks to any who may have inadvertently been overlooked in this list.

ILLUSTRATION CREDITS

Front cover: Photography Dana Ross with special effects by Grace Hauser and Derek Ruth
End sheets: Material courtesy Hollywood Bowl Museum, photography Peter Shamray
Title page: Donald Dietz, courtesy Los Angeles Philharmonic Archives
Rear cover: Antique postcard courtesy Cambria Archives

Los Angeles Philharmonic Archives: 9, 18R, 19R, 19B, 20T, 23, 25, 26, 27R, 36T, 42L, 59, 60, 82, 89, 90, 93, 94, 98L, 103, 107, 108, 115, 116R, 117, 119B, 123, 126, 129, 135

Robert Millard, courtesy Los Angeles Philharmonic Archives: 22T, 24, 27L, 28, 42L, 73, 86R, 118, 120T, 121, 124T, 132, 140, 141

Donald Dietz, courtesy Los Angeles Philharmonic Archives: 138, 142

David Weiss Photography, courtesy Los Angeles Philharmonic Archives: 67, 85, 92, 122, 126, 130, 134, 137

William J. Warren, courtesy Los Angeles Philharmonic Archives: 20B

Music Center Archives: 10T, 11, 12, 13, 14, 15, 16, 22B, 29, 35, 37, 41, 42R, 49B, 63, 64R, 66R, 78L, 88, 128

Music Center Archives/Otto Rothschild Collection: 4, 8, 18L, 19L, 21, 43, 55, 100, 113

Courtesy Hollywood Bowl Museum Collection: 7, 15, 30 (Corinne Grimaldi collection), 64L, 76, 78L, 84, 145

Courtesy Cambria Archives: 10B, 66L, 112, 114T, 146

Eric Wright, courtesy Getty Center for the History of Art and the Humanities: 31, 36B, 38, 39, 40

Frank O. Gehry and Associates: 44

Mark Lohman, courtesy Skidmore, Owings, and Merrill: 45

Toyo Miyatake: 46

Brookwell Photography: 49T

Courtesy Naima Prevots: 48, 52T

Archives for the Performing Arts, San Francisco: 52B

Courtesy Bella Lewitzky: 56

Courtesy of the Academy of Motion Picture Arts and Sciences: 74, 79, 80, 81, 83, 86L

By permission of Turner Entertainment Company: 74, 81, 83

Playboy Enterprises, Inc.: 95, 96

Ron Rogers: 97L

José Galvez for Playboy Enterprises, Inc.: 97R, 98R, 99

Caroline Greyshock, courtesy Bill Silva Presents: 104

Michael Jacobs/MJP, courtesy Bill Silva Presents: 109

Courtesy John Henken: 110

Courtesy Josef K. and Jo Ann Lesser: 116L, 129R

Index

First Printing
The Hollywood Bowl
© 1996 Los Angeles Philharmonic Association
Design by Kurt Hauser.
Imaging and production by Navigator Press.
Printed in Singapore.

Library of Congress
Catalogue Card Number: 95-080640
ISBN 0-9643119-2-5

SUMMER HOME OF THE LOS ANGELES PHILHARMONIC AND THE HOLLYWOOD BOWL ORCHESTRA

HOLLYWOOD BOWL

Glamorous Starlit

SYMPHONIES UNDER THE STARS

FIRST WEEK JULY 8-10-11-12

OFFICIAL PROGRAM 1930   PRICE 10¢

SUMMER SYMPHONY REVIEW

OFFICIAL PROGRAM

8TH SEASON 1929

HOLLYWOOD

BOWL

HOLLYWOOD BOWL

Los Angeles Times

FIFTH WAR LOAN

BOND SHOW

dram   FOURTH WEEK JULY 26-28
PRICE TEN CENTS

SEASON

L.A. PHILHARMONIC presents

HOLLYWOOD Bowl

Think Summer,
Think Music,
THINK HOLLYWOOD BOWL

SUMMER CON
1927

WILLIAM

50c

BALLE
RUSSE
de Monte Carlo

HOLLYWOOD BOWL

Holl

HOLLYWOOD BOWL
JULY 20, 21